"Dr. Ken Hemphill has once again provided a Biblical and practical resource. *Connected Community* reminds readers of the value and victory of the local church! Believers must give their lives to what Christ gave Himself for. This doctrinal resource issues a clarion call that is needed in the church of North America! There is hope for the church and *Connected Community* will help churches experience the joy of being on mission with Jesus as He builds His church!"

John Cross
Senior Pastor, South Biscayne Baptist Church

"Ken Hemphill has done Christendom a favor by reminding us again why the church is divinely important and eternally relevant. The chapter on church membership is worth the price of the book. Read it and you will be thankful for the church… and your church!"

James Merritt
Senior Pastor, Cross Pointe Church

CONNECTED COMMUNITY

OTHER BOOKS BY KEN HEMPHILL

Live it Up

The Bonsai Theory of Church Growth: Overcoming Artificial Barriers to Kingdom Growth

iBelieve Series
Core Convictions: Foundations of Faith

You Are Gifted: Your Spiritual Gifts and the Kingdom of God

I Am

Kingdom Promises Series

God Has	*God Is*	*But God*
God Will	*We Are*	*We Can*

SPLASH: Show People Love And Share Him

SPLASH 2: Discipleship

Eternal Impact: The Passion of Kingdom-Centered Communities

Making Change: A Transformational Guide to Christian Money Management

Parenting with Kingdom Purpose

EKG: The Heartbeat of God

The Prayer of Jesus Journal

The Prayer of Jesus: The Promise of Living in the Lord's Prayer

The Names of God

Ten Best Practices (to Make Your Sunday School Work)

All About Life

The Winning Spirit

Revitalizing the Sunday Morning Dinosaur

Serving God

The Antioch Effect: 8 Characteristics of Highly Effective Churches

Dr. Hemphill has several titles which are out of print. Some titles have been translated into various foreign langagues. Various kinds of tools for group study are available for *Prayer Of Jesus, EKG, Eternal Impact, Making Change, You Are Gifted, SPLASH, SPLASH 2* and *I Am*. See AuxanoPress.com.

i BELIEVE

CONNECTED COMMUNITY
BECOMING FAMILY THROUGH CHURCH

KEN HEMPHILL

Auxano
PRESS
Tigerville, South Carolina
www.AuxanoPress.com

ISBN 978-0-578-08165-6 (soft cover)
ISBN 978-0-578-08314-8 (hard cover)

Published by Auxano Press
Tigerville, South Carolina
www.AuxanoPress.com

All scripture quotations, unless otherwise indicated, are taken
from the New American Standard Bible®, Copyright © 1960, 1962,
1963, 1968, 1971, 1972, 1973, 1975, 1977, 1995 by The Lockman
Foundation. Used by permission. www.Lockman.org

To order additional copies, contact Ken Hemphill,
Auxano Press, P.O. Box 315, Tigerville, SC 29688;
or order online to www.auxanopress.com.

For additional resources for this and other studies, go to
www.auxanopress.com or contact Ken Hemphill,
Auxano Press, P.O. Box 315, Tigerville, SC 29688.

I joyfully dedicate this book
to our grandchildren.

Lois Kenzie Boesch

Emerson Cadden Oswald

Aubrey Dare Banks

R. M. Edward Oswald IV

Sloane Elizabeth Banks

Micah Ayden Boesch

Ruby Elspeth Oswald

Edie Katherine Banks

Your parents and your grandparents
have attempted to demonstrate
our love for Christ and His bride, the Church.
It is our prayer that you will excel in serving the King
through His earthly body the Church.

CONTENTS

ACKNOWLEDGMENTS

I have a lifelong love affair with the local church. My dad was a country pastor and many of my favorite memories are of church related events. I can still remember many of my early Sunday school teachers and the impact they had on my life. I remember with great fondness visiting our church members with my dad. Yes, I love the church.

The church has always had its critics and detractors, but it is facing new challenges in our day. Some persons argue that we are in the midst of a revolution. It has sometimes been called "churchless Christianity." Proponents argue that they are loyal followers of Christ but do not need the church to express their Christianity. Still others are redefining church in such a manner that it resembles little more than a few people sipping a latte and talking about Jesus. A third and more dangerous trend is apathetic church membership. For some today church is little more than a spiritual fraternity or a divine country club. I am praying that this book challenges such distortions and calls a new generation to a passionate relationship with the bride of Christ.

Paula, my wife and partner in ministry, continues to inspire and encourage. My children and their children are the context for most of what I have written. Tina and Brett, Rachael and Trey, Katie and Daniel are my children and my friends. I have dedicated this book to their children in the desire that love for the King and service to His church will be passed from generation to generation.

This is the second book in the "iBelieve" series by Auxano Press. Our goal is to provide biblically sound and reasonably priced tools to help individuals and their churches experience balanced growth. Kenneth Priest, Christi Butler, Judi Hayes, Emma Lou Savage, and Daphne Epting are wonderful friends and colleagues.

For the sake of simplicity and brevity, footnotes are few. I have been greatly blessed by many books on the church by men such as Robert Banks, F.J.A. Hort, Thabiti M. Anyabwile, Vincent Branick, Kevin DeYoung, Ted Kluck, Mark Dever, and Edmund Clowney. I am greatly indebted to these men, among many others, who have influenced my thinking concerning the church.

Free small group study helps for this book, *Connected Community*, are available online from AuxanoPress.com.

Ken Hemphill
Travelers Rest, South Carolina
Spring 2011

FOREWARD

There's no human relationship more important than that of a husband and wife. When centered on Christ, it's a relationship with profound meaning and purpose. It's love at the deepest human level. It gives us security and contentment and satisfaction. But it is demanding. It requires our energy and complete devotion. It must be intentionally cultivated. And it's a life-long commitment.

God, in His great wisdom, uses this special bond between a husband and wife to describe Christ's relationship with the Church, His bride. He loves us with a love that cannot be described. And in His love, He's entrusted us with a unique responsibility: He calls us to be His surrogate hands and feet; He commands us to love our neighbors; and He commissions us to do an important job – to spread the Gospel and make disciples all over the world. Now that's a tall order.

In *Connected Community*, Ken Hemphill takes us from that "Do you love me?" conversation between Jesus and Peter at the Sea of Galilee to the ultimate triumphant return of Christ and His Church in Jerusalem. And in between, he shares historical background and practical insights on being the Bride of Christ. May you be encouraged, challenged, and blessed by his thoughts.

Bryant Wright
Senior Pastor of Johnson Ferry Baptist Church
President of the Southern Baptist Convention

INTRODUCTION

"Do I have to go to church?" Every parent has heard that Sunday morning whine from their children. They are questioning the importance and value of getting out of bed early on Sunday morning and heading to church, which is often declared "boring." The problem is a little more complicated today, because the question is now being asked by people of every age group and every persuasion. This is no longer the question of the recalcitrant child; it is an issue being raised by people who would call themselves "committed evangelicals."

I recently required seminary students in my class to read a book on internet evangelism that was a compilation of papers presented at the "Internet Evangelism for the 21st Century" conference held in 2005 at Liberty University in Lynchburg, Virginia. One of the points made in several papers was that internet evangelism was critical because people have given up on the church.

Rowland Croucher stated, "They've given up on church. God is O.K. Jesus is O.K. But Church is psssh.... As of last year, George Barnet (sic. Barna) told us that more than 50% of committed evangelical Christians are not attending church. First time in history."[1]

David Bruce echoed the same theme citing Barna's statistics. "George Barna identified in this last five years that 10 million evangelicals have left the church. 10 million. Not just any evangelical, but evangelical lay leaders have left the church.... What George Barna has discovered is that people aren't just dropping out of church because they're not interested in going to church anymore; they're dropping out of church to do their own ministry."[2]

As I read through the book, I realized that this "do I have to go to church" theme was becoming a virtual refrain. Will Sampson confessed, "Well I have been a follower of Jesus my whole life. Last year I came to the point where if I didn't change something I was going to have to leave the church, because there's nothing left for me in the church (not upper case 'C' church, because I am deeply in love with the body of Christ)— the organized American church had little left for me. And so, for me, blogging has been a place to find other people. I'm one of the statistics. When David Bruce quotes statistics of people who are deeply committed to God but leaving the church, I'm one of them."[3]

A FEW CRITICAL QUESTIONS

This whole discussion raises several issues that I pray this study will answer. Does a Christian need church? Can I be part of the church with a capital 'C' and not belong to a local church? In case that distinction is confusing, some people claim to belong to the universal Church, the bride of Christ, but they have no relationship with any local church. Is that a viable option? Are we having church if a few couples gather at Starbucks for coffee, Bible study, and prayer? The recent interest in the house church movement has raised several questions related to what must transpire for believers to assemble as the church.

WILL IT DO ME ANY GOOD?

All of this discussion of the value of church reminds me of a somewhat humorous event that occurred in my first full-time pastorate. During the early weeks of my ministry, I decided to station myself in the drive-through area where most of our families entered the church. As soon as the car laden with children would pull to a stop, I would open the door for the wife and welcome the family to church. My welcoming strategy was not having the results I had anticipated. Often, when I opened the door a family would be discussing "deep theological issues" such as who left the quarterlies on the table or why it was necessary for the husband to sit in the driveway and blow the horn for five minutes while the wife dressed three children? A pastor's smiling face intruding into such weighty matters was a bit disconcerting for some of our families.

On the last Sunday before closing down this ill-fated project, God gave me a serendipitous event that caused me to think seriously about the purpose and effectiveness of church. I noticed a car waiting in the queue. Inside was a young lad about twelve and his father, a well-known and successful businessman in the community. The two were engaged in an intense dialogue—argument! As I watched, I began to guess about the content of their discussion. I had a few visual clues that helped. The young lad was dressed in his "going-to-church" best while his father had on a knit shirt and a golf hat. I surmised that their destinations were different. Dad was dropping off his son on his way to the golf course. As I opened the door, my suspicions were confirmed as I overheard the last three volleys in this verbal conflict.

"Dad, do you promise that you went to Sunday school and church when you were my age?"

Exasperated while looking anxiously at his watch, the father replied, "Son I never missed a Sunday when I was your age. Now get out of the car and go on in."

Dejected but not defeated, the son replied, "I'll go, but I bet you it won't do me any more good than it did you."

I had to ask myself what went on in this home that caused this boy to conclude that church had no impact on his dad? Second, I had to ask what was not happening in this church that caused a successful businessman to conclude that church was a good place for children but of little relevance to his own life?

Does church matter? Does it do us, our community, and our world any good?

---

1   Daniel Henrich (Ed). *Internet Evangelism in the 21st Century* (Handclasp International, 2007), p. 132.

2   Ibid. p. 18.

3   Ibid. p. 178.

CONNECTED COMMUNITY
THIS CHURCH BELONGS TO JESUS

Early in my pastoral ministry I wrote a book titled *The Official Rule Book for the New Church Game*. The title caused a few of my friends to insist, "But church is no game!" If they had taken time to read the first few pages, they would have discovered that this was precisely the point of the book and the title. My conviction is simple—no other earthly community or organization has the task, power, and significance as does the church. The key to the transformation of our culture and the redemption of the nations will depend upon the church becoming all she is intended to be.

More is at stake than we imagine! We cannot play at church; we cannot be casual about our church's mission or our involvement in its ministries. Christ is in love with His church. After all, it is His bride. He came to establish it, He died to redeem it, He was raised to empower it, He sent His Holy Spirit to indwell it, and He is coming again to bring it to himself. The church is the only earthly community which will continue to exist in heaven. Therefore our earthly investment through the church will have an eternal impact.

While I have used terms like organization and community to describe the church, I must insist that the church is no institution; it is a spiritual organism. It is organic in nature and therefore can never be seen as static but must be alive and growing. The church is the only community commissioned by God to change the world, advance the kingdom, and bring to victorious culmination the work of His Messiah. We are the most powerful force in the world!

THE FOUNDING CONFESSION (MATT. 16:13-20)

We cannot rightly understand what the church has become without first developing a clear understanding of its divine origin. The first use of the word church (*ecclesia*) comes from the lips of the Lord. Let's look first at the setting before we consider the implications of the term itself.

Jesus is in Caesarea Philippi. Jesus' question concerning current speculation about His true identity provides the setting for Peter's confession. When asked who the disciples believe Jesus to be, Peter, the spokesman of the twelve, dares to articulate what they have come to believe. "You are the Christ, the Son of the living God" (16:16). It is possible that we have read this text so often that we are immune to the radical nature of this confession. It is the singular declaration that will divide the Jewish world of the first century, setting brother against brother. It is the declaration that would shake Rome as men and women, boys and girls would boldly face persecution and death rather than recant on their declaration—"Jesus is Lord." It was radical then, it is radical now.

The word translated "Christ" in the English is nothing less than the affirmation that Jesus is the Messiah, "the anointed one," the King. The long-anticipated King from the line of David—the King who would usher in the eternal Kingdom of God, the King who would save His people from their sin—had made His appearance on earth. Can you even imagine what those first disciples must have thought and felt when Jesus gave His ringing confirmation to their boldest expectation—"Blessed are you, Simon Barjona, because flesh and blood did not reveal this to you, but My Father who is in heaven" (16:17)?

If we are going to restore the passion that will bring renewal to our churches, we must begin by recovering our awe of being part of the community established by the King of kings. We must fully commit to joining Him in His kingdom activity.

THE DRAMATIC ANNOUNCEMENT

The confession, "Jesus is Lord," is the high mark of this passage, but we cannot overlook the immediate declaration of the King—"I also say to you that you are Peter, and upon this rock I will build My church; and the gates of hell will not overpower it" (16:18). The connection between the Christ and His church is clear and dramatic. Christ's coming to earth is not simply to be understood in terms of our personal redemption, it must also be understood in terms of His mission to establish His redemptive community, His "church."

We too often treat our relationship with Christ as a purely personal matter as if we can live in dynamic relationship with Him apart from other believers who form His church. But the truth is, when we are "born again" we are "born into community." Christianity was designed to be lived out in community. To separate one's faith in Christ from dynamic life in His church is to strip it of God's chosen earthly expression. It is not an exaggeration to say that we cannot fully love Christ without loving His church.

Christ and His church are forever inextricably bound together. If we do not properly affirm that Jesus is the Son of God, the Messiah, we have no basis for asserting that the church is unique in origin, function, and authority. If Jesus is not fully God and the only means of redemption, the church is little more than a "divine country club." Thus it follows that if we do not whole-heartedly embrace the church as His earthly body, empowered to complete His mission, we have ignored God's plan for the reaching of the nations.

Let's pause to consider the significance of the word *ecclesia*, translated church. The word was commonly used to refer to the assembly of citizens of a Greek city (e.g. Acts 19:32). Citizens had privileged status over noncitizens and were called to assembly by a herald where they dealt with matters of common concern. Early Christians saw themselves as having special status as God's called out community, organized with the purpose of completing the Messianic mission. Paul speaks of this unique status in Ephesians 2:19. "…but you are fellow citizens with the saints, and are of God's household."

Perhaps of greater import is the use of the term *ecclesia* over one hundred times in the Greek translation of the Old Testament to translate the Hebrew word *qahal* which was regularly used for the gathering of the people of Israel, God's special covenant people. The early Christians were Jews who used the Greek translation of the Old Testament and thus the use of this particular word would have suggested that this "new community" had clear and unmistakable continuity with the Old Testament people of God. Thus the early Christians could speak of themselves as the true children of Israel (Romans 2:28-29) and as the people of the New Covenant prophesied in the Old Testament (Heb. 8:1-13).

Yet it was "new" in the sense that it was the prophesied rebuilding of the eternal kingdom of David which would include Jew and Gentile alike. This is the essence of James' argument in Acts 15:16 where he quotes from Amos 9:11. As God had purchased Israel as a community for Himself by redeeming them from Egypt, so God has purchased for Himself a new community by virtue of His Son's death and resurrection.

The word "church" is used in the New Testament as a reference to the entire people of God as it is in Matthew 16:18 and in Ephesians 1:22-23, where Paul declares that God gave Christ as head over all things "to the church". However it is most often used to refer to a local gathering of believers. Paul speaks of "the church of God which is at Corinth" (1 Cor. 1:2) or "the churches of Galatia" (Gal. 1:2). In the Corinthian passage, Paul immediately links this local church to the larger church by reminding them that they are one with "all who in every place call on the name of our Lord Jesus Christ." Simply stated, one cannot claim membership in the universal church without vital connection to a local expression of that global community of believers.

JESUS OWNS THE CHURCH AND INTENDS TO BUILD IT

We must not overlook the little pronoun "my." We have wrongly and foolishly taken ownership of Christ's church. When we acknowledge Christ as Lord or owner of the church, we will understand that He alone can determine its purpose and mission. We will cease bickering about what "I" want my church to be or do. The priority of the church as the singular instrument through which Christ will complete the task of discipling the nations (Matt. 28:19-20) was established by the resurrected Lord.

So let's pause to establish a working definition of church. *The church is a covenant community of born-again believers empowered by Christ for the advancing of the Kingdom through the discipling of all nations*. Does that definition describe the church you attend?

You may be thinking that your church is too small to have any real impact on the kingdom-sized task of discipling the nations. Wrong! Every church of every size and location is His church and thus has the same promise of His supernatural empowering. Your church is designed to grow. That doesn't necessarily mean it will keep getting larger and larger. Sometimes population shifts make such numerical growth unlikely, but it can grow through the planting of other churches and by joining with other like-minded churches in the reaching of the nations.

THE KEYS TO THE KINGDOM AND THE GATES OF HELL

The giving of the keys of the kingdom indicates that

there is an indissoluble union between the kingdom of God and His church. The church and the kingdom are not to be identified, but we may speak of the church as the visible representation of His kingdom on earth and also as His primary instrument of kingdom advance.

The stewardship of the keys of the kingdom enables the church to participate in the "binding" and "loosing" which occurs in heaven. "Keys" represent both authority and access. The keys are simply and yet profoundly the gospel of the kingdom which Jesus came to declare and to fulfill. Thus when the disciples confessed Jesus as Lord they entered the kingdom and as they proclaimed this truth, they opened the kingdom to all who would believe. Those who refused to hear and heed this message were closing the kingdom to themselves. The church today has the awesome privilege and responsibility of preaching the gospel and thus opening the door of faith to our neighbors and to the nations.

Another curious yet important phrase is "the gates of hell." This phrase indicates two fundamental truths about the church, about your church. If it is faithful to its mission it will face opposition. The devil doesn't want your church to grow and he can use either external pressure or internal dissension to keep the church from fulfilling its mission. Second, if it is steadfast it will be victorious.

When you read this familiar passage, you need to see your church moving victoriously into a world filled with evil, snatching people from the very gates of hell which are impotent to stand against the church. The term "gates of hell" like a similar "gates of Sheol" from the Old Testament both refer to death. Thus when Jesus assured the disciples that the "gates of hell" could not stand against them, He was indicating that the church will be victorious over death itself. Our message brings deliverance from death which is the consequence of sin. The church is the only earthly community which exists in heaven and thus it is eternal in nature. The things we do through the church have earthly meaning and eternal consequences.

Are you beginning to see church in a little different light? Do you treat the church with the same love Christ did? Do you value fellowship with other believers with the understanding that you will spend eternity together? Do you believe the ministries of the church have eternal impact? Do you believe that the needs of the lost have priority over the comfort of the saved?

CONNECTED COMMUNITY
GATHERED FOR WORSHIP

I had the privilege of studying in England for three years. Like most students and tourists, Paula and I made regular pilgrimages to Buckingham Palace, the home of British royalty. Sadly, I was never invited to have an audience with the Queen. I once asked my supervisor if he had met the Queen. With a tone of humble awe, he recounted his one fleeting visit to the palace and his audience with the Queen of England.

He was invited because he was a member of the team which had produced the New English Version of the Bible. Prior to his visit he was instructed concerning the appropriate dress and proper protocol when in the presence of the Queen. In spite of hours of rigorous and careful preparation, his entire visit lasted only a few moments as the Queen shook his hand and offered her heartfelt thanks for a job well done. Seeing my incredulity at his elaborate preparation for such a brief visit, he commented that no one would think of refusing an invitation from the Queen and no one would enter the presence of royalty without being thoroughly prepared.

Yet Christians, who have been invited into the very presence of the King of kings, often treat the gathering for corporate worship with casual disdain. Attendance is sometimes based on "how I feel," "who is preaching," or "what other options are available to me."

Our preparation for this glorious event is often casual, at best, or totally lacking as a late Saturday night leads to a hurried Sunday morning with a stressed out family whose attitude is anything but worshipful.

Have we forgotten that God has chosen to uniquely inhabit the praise of His people (Ps. 22:3)? Are we unaware that our earthly worship allows us to join with saints and angels in a heavenly festival of praise? The writer of Hebrews contrasts the awe Israel felt when God revealed Himself on Mount Sinai with the joyous celebration of God's new covenant people in worship. "But you have come to Mount Zion and to the city of the living God, the heavenly Jerusalem, and to myriads of angels, to the general assembly and church of the firstborn who are enrolled in heaven, and to God, the Judge of all, and to the spirits of the righteous made perfect, and to Jesus, the mediator of a new covenant, and to the sprinkled blood, which speaks better than the blood of Abel" (Heb. 12:22-24).

Can you imagine someone ignoring an invitation from the King to join in such a royal celebration?

THE PRIORITY OF WORSHIP AND THE PRESENCE OF THE KING

The majesty and glory of the Lord elicit worship. The Psalmist tells us that the heavens declare the glory of the Lord (Ps. 19:1). Thus it is appropriate that the Psalmist speaks of the heavens, the sun and the moon as offering praise to God (89:5, 148:3). If nature praises Him, how much more should man, created in His image, declare His glory? For that reason the Psalmist declares, "Because Your lovingkindness is better than life, My lips will praise You" (Ps. 63:3). He looks with anticipation to the day when, "All the earth will worship You and will sing praises to You" (66:4). The only place where praise to the One True King is not heard is in the pit of death and the despair of Sheol. "For Sheol cannot thank You, death cannot praise You; those who go down to the pit cannot hope for Your faithfulness" (Isa. 38:18).

Worship is a primary task of the church. It is the only appropriate response of the creature to the Creator. Worship is our passion, our joy, our source of empowering, and our call to evangelism and missions. It is not an overstatement to say that worship is the first calling and priority of the church. Authentic worship will prompt and prepare God's people to serve Him through the edification of fellow believers. Further, it will propel the worshipper to join God in the reaching of the nations so all peoples can join in worship of the One True King in preparation for eternal worship around His throne (Rev. 5:9-10).

The proliferation of "styles of worship" has recently led to what some have called "worship wars." These wars, concerning worship styles, have frequently led to church splits or angry members vowing not to return to worship. What a tragedy! Debates that center on worship styles demonstrate our failure to think biblically about the true nature of worship. All too often we evaluate worship based on what it did for us. Here's a news flash—Worship is not about us! We are not the audience. God is both the object and the audience of true worship and He delights in the praise of His people.

Authentic worship is not about the beat or style of the music, nor is it about the performance of the choir, soloist, or praise team. We are all the praise team! It is not about illuminating power point presentations, nor entertaining dramatic skits, it is about the believer's passionate desire to encounter and know God. While all of these elements may be used in worship, they must not be worshipped. They have authenticity only when they serve to lead us to worship God.

Corporate worship should properly flow from personal worship, but personal worship will never replace the need for corporate worship. Two points need to be considered. If you see corporate worship as boring then you should look first at the quality of your own personal worship. Second, a true worshipper will never attempt to substitute personal worship for the privilege of joining with fellow-believers in corporate worship, an earthly event which allows us to join our voices with the angels and the firstborn assembled in heaven (Heb. 12:22-24).

In writing to the Corinthians, on two separate occasions Paul speaks of the necessity of the whole church gathering for worship. It is likely that the church in Corinth was composed on numerous small gatherings which met throughout the city. These small gatherings would be comparable to our small groups today. Nonetheless, these "house churches" or "small groups" were required to come together for city wide corporate events.

The first mention of a corporate gathering for worship is found in 1 Corinthians 11, when the church gathered to celebrate the Lord's Supper—"Therefore when you meet together, it is not to eat the Lord's Supper" (20). Their lack of concern for the poorer members and the resulting disunity has led them to "despise the church of God" (22) and thus what transpired could not be called "the Lord's Supper". A second mention is found in 1 Corinthians 14:23—"Therefore if the whole church assembles together…." The entire fourteenth chapter is about the matter of corporate worship and who may speak and in what context. The key thought of chapter fourteen is that all must be done with concern for the edification of the believer and the reaching of the unbeliever. For our purposes, it is important that we underline the critical nature of corporate worship for the life of the church and the growth of the individual believer.

The writer to the Hebrews gives a strong word of warning to those who are tempted to ignore corporate worship. It would be helpful to read Hebrews 10:19-25 in its entirety. The author speaks of the privilege of worship which was made possible by the blood of Jesus. He then repeats the phrase "let us" three times. In the first instance he speaks of drawing near with a clean conscience, secondly he speaks of holding fast the confession of our faith, and finally he speaks of stimulating one another to love and good deeds. Listen carefully to the final reminder—"not forsaking our own assembling together, as is the habit of some, but encouraging one another" (10:25a).

Worship not only allows us to worship holy God, it enables us to grow in our faith and encourage others.

THE ELEMENTS OF BIBLICAL WORSHIP

Proclamation, praise, and prayer are three key elements which should be prioritized in every corporate worship experience. These three elements will, in turn, lead to the edification of the saints and the evangelization of the world.

Proclamation of the word. Worship is not to be viewed as a pageant or a performance of a professional speaker who is paid to air his opinions on stress reduction, self-actualization, or social needs, nor is it to be treated as group therapy. Since worship is about God, His word must be central. Edmund Clowney writes, "The heart of spiritual worship is hearing what the Lord says to us, responding to Him in prayer and praise, and encouraging one another in his fellowship."[1]

The reading and proclamation of God's word and the congregation's response to that word is the centerpiece of worship. Preaching addresses God's people in God's presence with God's word. The public reading of God's word and expositional preaching of that word must never be diminished by any other element of worship, but must be the stack pole from which all else flows.

Preaching is declaring the truth of God in the power of the Holy Spirit. Paul writes to the Corinthians concerning the priority of preaching in the first two chapters of 1 Corinthians. The Jews were clamoring for signs—some spectacular evidence of God's power (1:22). The Greeks longed for philosophical wisdom (1:22). Paul declares, "but we preach Christ crucified, to Jews a stumbling block and to Gentiles foolishness, but to those who are the called, both Jews and Greeks, Christ the power of God and the wisdom of God" (1:23-24). Is it any wonder that later in life Paul would charge young Timothy to "preach the word; be ready in season and out of season; reprove, rebuke, exhort, with great patience and instruction" (2 Tim. 4:2)?

We must never underestimate the power of God's Word to convert the sinner and transform the saved.

Praise through song. The joyous singing of God's people in His presence and for His goodness is an element clearly seen in Old Testament worship and continued in the New. A wonderful example of a spontaneous hymn of praise is found in Exodus 15 where Moses leads the sons of Israel as they celebrate the greatness of God who has delivered them from the hand of the Pharaoh. Just listen—"The Lord is my strength and song, and He has become my salvation; This is my God, and I will praise Him; My father's God, and I will extol Him" (15:2).

Music provides us with a means of praising, praying, proclaiming, and edifying others. Music, for many, is the central thread which knits the various elements of worship together. Music should be selected based primarily on its biblical content, but attention should be given to its suitability for leading the congregation to focus on and adore God. The style might vary from context to context, but it should always be theologically sound and culturally suitable.

Prayer. Prayer was central to both Old and New Testament worship, but is often an afterthought in the modern day service. In fact, it was so central to synagogue worship that it could be referred to as "a place of prayer" (Acts 16:13). We would do well to remember that Jesus cleansed the Temple because the Jews of His day had failed to treat the temple as a "house of prayer for all the nations" (Mark 11:17).

Prayer provides the opportunity for us to come boldly before the throne of grace. It permits us to verbally acknowledge God's presence, to confess our sins, to seek His forgiveness, to stand before Him in praise, to offer ourselves to God, to ask for His provision, to intercede for others, and to offer thanksgiving to our gracious King. Prayer often provides an excellent barometer, measuring the spiritual condition of a congregation.

The offering of ourselves. The offering was a high point of worship both for Israel and the New Testament church. It was a time for the recognition of God's ownership, human stewardship, and the graciousness of all of life. Worship through offering should never be interpreted as the means for subscribing a budget, but as the God given vehicle for expressing our dependence on God and our gratitude for His loving provision. The giving of His tithe and our offerings is a normative sacrifice as is our praise and our good deeds (Heb. 13:15-16). In some cases, we have divorced financial stewardship from its theological foundation so that we have made the time of offering as little more than a punch line to a joke about it being an essential element of a church meeting.

The offering is not complete until we offer ourselves as a living sacrifice (Rom. 12:1-2). For that reason, we should all be prepared to respond to God's invitation provided through the preaching of His word. Each time we hear God's word declared, we should desire to respond with Isaiah, "Here am I. Send me!" (6:8).

WORSHIP AND MISSIONS

The ultimate evaluation of the vitality of our worship will be seen in our commitment to God's mission. Worship is central to a kingdom centered church because it flows out of our devotion to the King and provides the passion and power that enables each church to extend its ministry to the ends of the earth. As we read the book of Acts we are drawn time and again to the church at Antioch. This is the church responsible for sending Paul and Barnabas for the reaching of the nations. How does a church develop such an intense mission passion that it sends its best leaders into the fields that are ripe for harvest? A quick glance at that church at worship will give you the key. "While they were ministering to the Lord and fasting, the Holy Spirit said, 'Set apart for Me Barnabas and Saul for the work to which I have called them'" (13:2). The word translated "ministering" is *leitergeo*, from which we get the English word *liturgy*. They were worshipping!

Authentic worship tunes our hearts to the Heart of God. As a result true worship always calls the believer to meaningful service (Rom. 12:1-2) and intentional missions (Acts 13:2).

---

1   Edmund P. Clowney, *The Church* (Illinois; InterVarsity Press, 1995), p. 124.

CONNECTED COMMUNITY
ON MISSION WITH THE KING

The Lord calls His church to worship Him and commissions and empowers it to take His message to the ends of the earth before His return so that all nations and people groups can join in worship when the church assembles in the heavenlies. This statement of mission or purpose seems so simple and so biblical you would think it would find general consensus among all those persons who consider themselves to be part of the church of the Lord Jesus Christ. Not so!

In the '60s, the World Council of Churches, working from a servant church model, redefined the mission of the church. At the 1966 World Conference on the Church and Society in Geneva, it was determined that the work of the church was the liberation of the oppressed. Thus the mission of the church was to support revolutionary movements by participating in them and bear witness from within.[1] Thus the church's mission was redefined as a struggle for political justice. At the WCC Assembly in Canberra in 1991, newer concerns such as feminism, environmentalism, and other religions were considered. The Report called for exploring non-violence for the transformation of society. Systemic evil was identified as existing world economies and ecological destruction. The Report called for dialogue with non-Christian religions. While affirming that salvation is in Christ, it indicates that it is not only in Him. Those attending affirmed: "We seek also to remain open to other people's expression of truth as they have experienced it."[2]

Is the church called to save our planet or our community by pursuing a political and ecological agenda? Are we to join in wars of liberation for the afflicted and oppressed? Are we to pursue dialogue with other world religions to establish common ground and thus promote understanding and world peace? Our answer to such questions must reflect the passion of our Lord who gave His life to establish the church, sent His Spirit to infill it, and thus declares it to be His bride and His body. In short, our answer must be biblically sound.

THE GOSPEL MANDATES MISSION

The Bible from Genesis to Revelation clearly teaches that man's problem begins with the heart. The Psalmist declares; "The fool has said in his heart, 'There is no God.' They are corrupt, they have committed abominable deeds; there is no one who does good" (Ps. 14:1). This single verse summarizes man's ultimate problem. He is in outright rebellion against His Creator. This rebellion leads to sin and that sin ultimately leads to separation from God who is by nature "holy." Sin is the single universal problem which unites all of mankind. In the book of Romans, Paul declares that Jew and Gentile alike are all under sin (3:9). He then cites numerous Old Testament references to make his case which is simply summarized in a single sentence—"For all have sinned and fall short of the glory of God" (3:23).

The results of the sin problem of man and its solution are stated in the same verse—"For the wages of sin is death, but the free gift of God is eternal life in Christ Jesus our Lord" (Rom. 6:23). Man can do nothing to save himself since he is spiritually bankrupt (dead) and separated from holy God. But listen to the Good News (gospel)—"being justified as a gift by His grace through the redemption which is in Christ Jesus; whom God displayed publicly as a propitiation in His blood through faith" (Rom. 3:24-25a). Holy God chose to bear our sin, providing for our righteousness, and giving us new natures (cf. 2 Cor. 5:17). What an incredible truth—God reconciled us to Himself through Christ (2 Cor. 5:18). Man is "justified as a gift by His grace through the redemption which is in Christ Jesus" (Rom. 3:24). Man cannot earn that which is a gift, he can only receive it by faith—"For by grace you have been saved through faith; and that not of yourselves, it is the gift of God" (Eph. 2:8).

The gospel truly is good news. It is incredible news! Sinful man can be reconciled to holy God by receiving the grace gift of God which was provided in the sending of His Son. "For God so loved the world; that He gave His only begotten Son, that whoever believes in Him shall not perish, but have eternal life" (John 3:16).

Do you believe that message? Have you experienced the new birth? If so you will be driven by the enormity of grace to declare that message. We looked earlier at 2 Corinthians 5:17-18 which told us we could be new creatures by being reconciled to God through Christ. Now read the last half of verse 18—"and gave us the ministry of reconciliation." Paul continues—"Therefore, we are ambassadors for Christ, as though God were making an appeal through us; we beg you on behalf of Christ, be reconciled to God" (2 Cor. 5:20).

The gospel mandates mission! The gospel alone deals with man's most critical need! When the gospel is ignored mission is lost, when mission is lost the gospel is ignored. The transformation of the individual heart can lead to the transformation of society, but the reverse is not true. Thus while the church may do many things and provide many ministries to solve personal needs and resolve social ills, it must always do these with a focus on its mission—to declare the gospel that Jesus saves.

JESUS CALLED DISCIPLES TO BE ON MISSION WITH HIM

Our first glimpse of Jesus' earthly strategy for advancing His kingdom is found in Matthew 4:18-22. While Jesus ministered to the multitudes, He called out some men to join Him in His kingdom activity. His call was simple and yet profound—"Follow Me, and I will make you fishers of men." The requirement on their part is to follow Christ. The work He will accomplish in and through them is stated in language these men would have readily understood. The first two, Peter and Andrew, were fishermen. Jesus' mission was to save the lost (1 Tim. 1:15) and His plan for the continuation of this ministry was to make missionaries of His followers.

In His inaugural message, the Sermon on the Mount, Jesus indicates that those who follow Him will be salt and light (Matt. 5:13-16). As salt their lifestyle will bring flavor to a tasteless world. As light they will bring illumination that will clarify that their good deeds come from the Father and thus will lead men to give glory to God alone. Salt and light speak to lifestyle and witness which must always be bound together in the life of those who follow Christ.

Notice that followers of Jesus are by their very nature salt and light. We do not choose to be salt and light; on the contrary we are chosen by Christ and are given His nature enabling us to be salt and light. It would be contrary to the nature of salt to be tasteless and against the nature of light not to bring illumination. Salt and light are who we are before it is what we do!

After the disciples had been following Jesus for a period of time, He allowed them to see the world through His eyes. "Seeing the people, He felt compassion for them, because they were distressed and dispirited like sheep without a shepherd" (Matt. 9:36). His passion for a lost and hurting world can be felt as He declares that the harvest is plentiful but the workers are few (9:37). After instructing the disciples to pray that the Lord would thrust out workers into the harvest, Jesus sends them out to participate in the very activities they had seen Him doing (Matt. 10:1-15). They have now become gatherers in the harvest with Him.

This ministry of harvesting is so essential to following Jesus that He declares, "He who is not with Me is against Me; and He who does not gather with Me scatters" (Matt. 12:30, Lk. 11:23). A missional lifestyle is not an option for the church or its individual members.

If we are not gathering with Him, we are scattering and that places us in the category of those who are against Him.

A missional lifestyle is no minor chord in the life and teaching of Jesus. Luke tells us that tax collectors and sinners were coming to Jesus. The religious establishment of His days, represented by the Pharisees and scribes, were grumbling about Jesus' propensity to associate with sinners. Jesus tells three parables all dealing with lost items (a sheep, a coin, and a son). The first two parables end with the searcher finding the lost item and a celebration which is compared to the heavenly celebration that occurs when a sinner repents. In the last story the young prodigal is forced to find his way home by himself. Once again there is a party, but on this occasion the elder son remains stubbornly outside. The elder brother, like the religious establishment of Jesus' day, had become proud of his religious service but had failed to understand his father's desire that every prodigal be found. The elder brother was a scatterer rather than a gatherer. He had neglected his missional calling.

Many churches could well be named "The Elder Brother _____ Church." They are busy obeying commands and tending the programs of the church, but have failed to express any concern or devise any plan for reaching the prodigals around them.

THE CONSTITUTION AND COMMISSIONING OF THE CHURCH

When the disciples first confess that they believe Jesus is the Messiah (Matt. 16:13-20), He declares His strategy for the advance of His kingdom. He will build His church and give it the keys of the kingdom and the authority to advance against the very gates of Hades.

The pronoun "My" speaks to ownership and intimacy. The church belongs to Him and thus He alone has the authority to determine its purpose. He indwells His church through His Spirit, thus giving it life and vitality. Christ's mission will be continued and completed by His church. The "keys of the kingdom" speak of the authority and message of the church, which is the good news of Christ. It is this message that gives the church authority over the gates of Hades, which represents death and eternal separation from God.

At this point Jesus warns His disciples that it is not yet the time to reveal that He is the Messiah. Messianic speculation was rampant and for most people it had political overtones. Jesus reveals to His disciples "the rest of the story." He must go to Jerusalem and suffer many things leading to His death and resurrection. It is the death of the Messiah that provides the way of redemption thus constituting the church and it is His resurrection which provides for the descent of the Spirit thus empowering the church.

If we fast forward to the end of Matthew's gospel, we can link the constitution of the church with the commissioning of the church. When the disciples encountered the resurrected Lord, they worshipped Him, even though some remained doubtful. Jesus tells them that He now has received all authority in heaven and in earth (Matt. 28:16-20). Paul speaks to this authority in Ephesians 1:20-23, declaring that God has seated Christ at His right hand far above all rule and authority and power and dominion. He has placed everything in subjection under Him and made Him as head over all things so that the church might express His fullness.

Based on His supreme authority, Christ commands His disciples—"Go therefore and make disciples of all the nations, baptizing them in the name of the Father and the Son and the Holy Spirit, teaching them to observe all that I commanded you; and lo, I am with you always, even to the end of the age" (Matt. 28:19-20). The imperative is "make disciples." The extent of our disciple-making is "all nations." Our mission strategy is defined by the participles "going," "baptizing," and "teaching." The task is universal in its scope and timeless in its application. The great commission is an imperative not a suggestion.

We can fast-forward once more and join the disciples and the resurrected Lord in His final earthly appearances. Luke, the author of Acts tells us that Jesus appeared to the disciples on several occasions over forty days teaching them about the kingdom of God (Acts 1:3). Gathering them one final time, He told them to wait until they are baptized and empowered by the Spirit. Tragically, some disciples are still focused on the political kingdom of Israel (1:6). Jesus refocuses them by reminding them of their empowering and mission. "But you will receive power when the Holy Spirit has come upon you; and you shall be My witnesses both in Jerusalem, and in all Judea and Samaria, and even to the remotest part of the earth" (Acts 1:8). Notice again, witness is who we are before it becomes what we do!

THE GREAT TRAGEDY

We began this section with a look at the World Council of Churches' attempt to redefine the mission of the church. No doubt most persons reading this book would agree that such a redefinition is unbiblical and distorted. Neither the WCC nor your local church has the authority to redefine the mission of the church. The tragedy is that some Bible believing churches affirm the Great Commission in theory but fail to implement it in reality. When a congregation ignores its God-given mission it loses its direction, begins to atrophy, and begins to be shattered by internal dissension. When a church loses sight of its mission it ceases to be the church.

The church may use many strategies for the fulfilling of the Great Commission. They may offer literacy classes, adopt a school, work with issues of poverty and drug abuse, help people with financial needs and car repairs, organize sports leagues, provide a collection point for recycling, and implement many other such caring ministries. But all of these must be done with our unique mission in mind. No one else has the message of life and we must never lose sight of it as we are offering a cup of cold water in His name.

1   Edmund P. Clowney, *The Church* (Illinois: Downers Grove, 1995) p. 156.
2   From the 'Report of the Report Committee', *Ecumenical Review* 43:2. April 1991 III: 75, cited in Clowney, p. 157.

CONNECTED COMMUNITY

I BELONG

We might as well address the proverbial 500-pound gorilla in the room. Is church membership necessary? The lack of interest in church membership is a natural byproduct of those who espouse a "churchless Christianity." This is the "I-love-Jesus-but-I-don't-need-the-church" crowd.

Some people see church membership as a secondary issue. They treat it as a quaint and slightly outdated proposition of a bygone era when church membership was a cultural necessity. After all, it would be difficult to sell insurance, cars, funeral plots, etc. in a small community unless one was in good standing with a local church.

Some people want to be involved in a church without going through the process of joining, which often requires a rite of entry such as baptism, a membership class, or a covenant. Is this "let's-just-enjoy-the-benefits-without-membership-option" any different from couples who choose to live together without the traditional commitment of marriage? These couples see traditional marriage as a secondary matter as long as they're in a committed, loving relationship.

Still other people see membership at one particular church as a hindrance to their spiritual freedom and personal development. They argue that they are "part of" several local churches. They attend one church for the music and preaching, another for youth or children activities, and still another for a men's or ladies' Bible study. They may even say they belong to the "universal church" but do not want to be tied to any "local church."

The underlying theme in all the scenarios presented above is that they are self-centered and not Christ-centered or kingdom-focused. The central question being asked by many is "what is best or most convenient for me and my family?" Many modern day options are a thinly disguised excuse for the unwillingness to make a commitment and be held accountable.

I want to change the question from "is church membership necessary?" to "is church membership biblical?" If it is a biblical norm, then it is a Christian responsibility and privilege. Does the Bible teach church membership? I would agree that it would take exegetical gymnastics to point to a single "proof text" that declares that one must join a church. Yet I think the pattern of responsible church membership is clearly and consistently taught throughout the New Testament.

THE PATTERN ESTABLISHED IN ACTS

The book of Acts' purpose is to demonstrate the activity of the Holy Spirit through the apostles as they are obedient to the task assigned them as witnesses beginning in Jerusalem and extending to the ends of the earth (Acts. 1:8). A brief survey of the book will demonstrate that the strategy of the Holy Spirit was to establish communities of believers (churches) throughout the known world. The advance of the kingdom on earth depends upon a church planting strategy because the church is the visible body of Christ on earth and the chosen instrument for kingdom advance.

The Birth of the Church

It is fair to say that Pentecost was the birthday of the church. Peter's message and call to repentance had such a profound impact that 3,000 souls were added that day (Acts 2:41). We must ask "added to what" or, rather, "to whom." The context makes it clear that these 3,000 persons were added to the existing believers in such a manner that they formed a distinct community where apostolic teaching, unique fellowship expressed in a tangible way, unity, and worship became the norm (2:43-47). The phrase—added to their number—is repeated again in 2:47 and 5:14. The emphasis on "numbers" is not simply a means of demonstrating the vitality of the early church; it is an indication that there existed some means of keeping track of those persons who were part of this growing community of believers.

Peter and John are arrested for preaching and are taken before the chief priests and elders to be examined (Acts 4). Since the authorities cannot deny the visible evidence that has accompanied the preaching of the apostles, they threaten and release them. When released, Peter and John go to the place where their own "companions" are gathered. They give a report to a group of believers who are gathered at a place clearly known to them.

This event is followed by a summary statement (4:32-37) that is similar to 2:43-47. This Spirit-filled community continues to express fellowship by providing for one another's needs to such an extent that there was not a needy person among them. The word rendered "congregation" used in 4:32 had acquired the sense of a civic or religious community in other first century writings. The use of this word indicates that the early believers are developing both structure and identity.

The First Use of the Word "Church" in Acts

This story of sacrificial giving and community living is followed by the tragic story of the deceit of Ananias and Sapphira, who pledged a piece of property and then failed to give the full sale price of the property. As a result, both husband and wife died. The result— "Great fear came over the whole church, and over all who heard of these things" (5:11).

This is the first use of the word "church" (*ecclesia*) in Acts. This word was used by Jesus in Matthew 16:18 when He announced His intention to build His own church. The Greek word has both a Gentile and Jewish background. In secular Greek it denotes the gathering of citizens of a Greek city (cf. Acts 19:32). Its Jewish background is more significant to us. When the Old Testament was translated into Greek (Septuagint), *ecclesia* was used to denote the Jewish people as the "congregation of Yahweh." The use of this word leaves little doubt that we are now dealing with a group of people who are bound together in such a manner that they comprise an identifiable community with both rights and responsibilities.

The Developing Structure of the Church

Chapter six provides a clear indication of identifiable leadership, structure, and community participation. The growth of the church creates a crisis which becomes an opportunity. The congregation was providing support for the needy widows. These women may have been abandoned by their Jewish family when they became followers of Christ. The twelve, who are clearly the leaders of the church in Jerusalem, summon the congregation and ask them to select men who would be qualified to take care of the widows (3). The congregation selected seven men for this task and brought them before the apostles who commissioned them (5-6). A process for congregational decision making is clearly developing.

The Scattering of the Church

The success of the church leads to persecution and the scattering of the believers. Saul is not content to drive the Christians out of Jerusalem, he desires to pursue these followers of "the Way" and bring them back to Jerusalem for imprisonment (9:1-3). The name—"the Way"—is found again in 19:9, 23, 22:4, 24:14, 22. It is likely that this term was used by the early Christians to denote their movement as a way of life or redemption. It may well have been a clear echo of Jesus statement in John 14:6. Clearly, by this early date a group of people exist who are identifiable to those within and those without the group.

Some of the persons scattered by the persecution came to Antioch and preached the Lord Jesus to both Jews and Greeks. The news of the large number of converts in Antioch soon reached the ears of the church in Jerusalem who sent Barnabas to Antioch (11:21-22). Barnabas was sent as an "official" representative of the mother church in Jerusalem. We see a growing sense of the need for doctrinal accountability as the Spirit grows the church in areas beyond Jerusalem.

Barnabas, in turn, brings Saul to Antioch. "And for an entire year they met with the church and taught considerable numbers; and the disciples were first called Christians in Antioch" (11:26). Most commentators believe this name was applied to early followers of Christ by the pagans of Antioch. While Christ (*Christos*) would be the name of an office to the Greek-speaking Jews, to the pagans of Antioch it was the name of the man of whom these people were always talking. Thus they called them the Christ-people, the Christians.

The verb translated "were called" literally means to "transact business" under a particular name. This has led some scholars to argue that the Christians applied this name to themselves.[1] In either case, we can clearly see that groups of people in various locations could now be identified as belonging to Christ. They met together for worship and fellowship, were held accountable for the integrity of their teaching, had identifiable leaders, and desired to convince others to join their movement.

The story of the church in Antioch continues in Acts 13:1-3. Verse one indicates that a clearly defined leadership structure had been established. The second verse indicates that a pattern of worship and prayer was practiced by the members of the community.

In the third verse the believers in Antioch respond to the urging of the Spirit by commissioning Paul and Barnabas to begin a church planting movement. The repeated reference to "they" indicates this was a decision ratified by the whole church and thus it is appropriate that when the missionaries return to Antioch, they make their report to the whole church (14:26ff). Luke tells us that Paul and Barnabas not only planted churches, but they also appointed leaders in every church to facilitate continued growth (14:23).

The Council in Jerusalem

The success of the Gentile ministry created a situation that demanded doctrinal clarification. The question— "Must a Gentile be circumcised to be saved?" Since the church at Antioch commissioned Paul and Barnabas for their mission trip they sent them along with "some others" to Jerusalem to clarify the matter. Luke specifies that these men were sent "by the church" (15:3). When they arrive in Jerusalem they are received "by the church and the apostles and the elders" (15:4).

After a time of lively discussion, a decision is made. It seemed good to the leaders and the whole church to choose men and send them to Antioch with a letter detailing the decision reached by those meeting in Jerusalem. When they arrived in Antioch, they "gathered the congregation together" and delivered the letter (15:30). Later Paul and Timothy revisit several established churches and deliver the decrees decided upon in Jerusalem (16:4). Not only do we see clearly defined local churches, but we also see a linking together of these churches for mutual support and accountability.

As the Acts' account progresses, we learn that these early communities developed a consistent pattern of gathering on the first day of the week to worship, distinguishing them from the Jews who gathered on the Sabbath (20:7). The leaders of various churches are known and thus can be encouraged to care for and give administrative oversight to those whom the Holy Spirit has placed in their charge (20:28).

THE LETTERS TO THE CHURCHES

The Pauline letters are a strong testimony to the existence of established churches with a membership who could be called together to hear and respond to the teaching of their founding apostle. Someone had to receive the letter, summon the church to hear the letter, and then report again to Paul about the response to the letter. These letters were later collected, shared, and preserved by these same churches.

1 Corinthians 1:2 not only speaks of the church of God which is at Corinth, it further indicates that Paul understands that this letter may be read by other "saints by calling" who are in other places. In this particular letter, Paul speaks of a sin of sexual immorality which is not even practiced among the Gentiles (5:1). Paul gives instructions that when they "are assembled" they should follow his instructions and "deliver such a one to Satan," which means put him outside the assembly. We can conclude that discipline and accountability were exercised by the early church. It is possible that 2 Corinthians 2:5-11 speaks of the reinstatement of the brother who had been punished by the majority (2:6). The word "majority" seems to indicate that some voting

process was in place in the early church and that membership could be revoked and restored.

In 1 Corinthians 11 Paul gives instructions for women who want to speak in the assembly. His final appeal in this section is that all must abide by the practice agreed upon by other "churches of God" (11:16). In that same chapter he speaks about the gathering of the believers as the church. "For, in the first place, when you come together as a church, I hear that divisions exist among you" (11:18). He proceeds to give instructions on celebrating the Lord's Supper.

Chapters 12-14 contain explicit instructions on the use of spiritual gifts in the assembly. The specificity of the instructions in ch. 14 again indicates that the church met regularly for worship. Further, it demonstrates that unbelievers could be found in the assembly. While many people could participate by using their gifts, control could be exercised and those with the wrong attitude could be prohibited from speaking.

In chapter 16 Paul gives specific directions about the collection for the saints in Jerusalem. "On the first day of every week each one of you is to put aside and save, as he may prosper, so that no collections be made when I come" (16:2). Notice again the meeting is on Sunday and regular giving was anticipated. When Paul arrives he will receive the offering and accompany "whomever you may approve" to take the offering to Jerusalem (3).

He concludes the letter with affirmation of their leaders and instruction that they are in subjection to such men (16). Finally, Paul conveys greetings from the churches of Asia and the church meeting in the house of Aquila and Prisca (19) to the believers in Corinth.

Even a cursory glance at the other Pauline letters will reveal a similar pattern. Galatians is addressed "to the churches of Galatia" which suggests that several churches were linked together for encouragement. It is likely that Ephesians and Colossians were addressed to the churches of pro-Consular Asia, possibly the seven churches mentioned in the book of Revelation. In the various Pauline letters, you will find the mention of identifiable leaders as well as specific instructions which are to be read and obeyed.

In 1 and 2 Timothy, Paul passes the baton of leadership to Timothy. These two letters give specific instruction about church organization and structure, including such matters as the qualifications for overseers and deacons. He even speaks of the matter of compensation for those who work hard at preaching and teaching (5:17-18). The phrase "double honor" must be understood in terms of financial compensation in the light of the reference to "muzzling the ox" in verse 18. Thus a paid staff has now developed.

In 1 Timothy 5 Paul gives instruction about the ongoing care of the widows. Notice the specificity of the instructions in 5:9—"A widow is to be put on the list only if she is not less than sixty years old, having been the wife of one man…." There is a list of approved widows which is kept by the church.

CONCLUSION

The evidence of the entire New Testament points to an identifiable body of believers who joined themselves together for worship and for mutual encouragement. Their worship included the participation of many gifted persons. They received offerings, commissioned missionaries, received reports, visits, and letters from various leaders, were expected to abide by the traditions established by the churches, and were called upon to pray and support others in churches like their own.

There can be little question that first century believers were expected to participate fully in a local fellowship of believers which we can, without hesitation, call a church. Paul indicates that it is the work of the Spirit which immerses believers into the life of the body. "For by one Spirit we were all baptized into one body, whether Jews or Greeks, whether slaves or free, and we were all made to drink of one Spirit" (1 Cor. 12:13). When a person is truly born again, he/she will express that new birth by fully identifying with a community of believers as the result of the work of the Spirit in his/her life.

But the issue is not merely one of "joining a church." The issue is one of a covenant commitment that includes worship, hearing and responding to Gods' Word, involvement in the mission of the church, and a financial investment in the mission of the church. Perhaps a larger problem than "churchless Christianity" is "token churchianity without commitment."

---

1   For additional information see F.F. Bruce, *The Book of Acts* (Michigan: Eerdmans, 1960), p. 241 and footnote 26.

CONNECTED COMMUNITY
NO ORPHANS HERE

I grew up in Thomasville, North Carolina, the home of Mills Home Orphanage. The "orphans," as we called them back then, attended public school. I developed friendships with several young men from Mills Home and our family often invited an "orphan" home for the weekend. My parents treated my friends as family and not guests.

One Sunday afternoon we were returning our orphan to the beautiful Mills Home campus. There were several baseball diamonds, a gym, a swimming pool, horses, and lots of playmates. I remarked to my friend, "You've got it made—lots of activities and plenty of friends. What else could you want?" With a note of sadness in his voice he replied, "A father like yours and a family. I am an orphan." For the first time in my young life I began to understand the value of family.

Words like loneliness, isolation, and alienation occur frequently in print and in song today. We have become a transient nation, and many people feel like they are simply a number, a statistic, with no roots and no real sense of family.

I was pastor of First, Norfolk for nine years. It was a wonderfully friendly church. The lobby was always a beehive of activity as people shook hands and hugged one another. One Sunday I was preaching on church as family and I used the illustration of the family reunion which occurred in the lobby every Sunday. A lady approached me after the service and indicated that all the activity in the lobby made her feel even more isolated. She came to church alone and had not developed any close friendships. She stood alone watching all the frenzied activity wishing that someone would speak to her and, at the same time, fearing that someone would speak to her. How do we truly become family so that everyone feels that they are an integral part of the household of God?

In Ephesians 2:19-22 Paul uses three images to describe the church—fellow-citizens with the saints, God's household, and a building structured and put together by God. The image of citizenship underlines the legal rights of a citizen, treasured in the first century. The image of a building focuses on the organic nature of the church, designed by God as a dwelling place for His Spirit on earth. The phrase "God's household" is the most intimate and speaks of the church as the family of God.

The church is no mere institution to be compared with other earthly institutions. It has the legal right of kingdom citizenship, the nurturing fellowship of family, and the divine empowering of the Spirit.

Too much is at stake for us to ever play church, treating it as little more than a religious social club or a holy huddle. The church is not a voluntary organization of like-minded friends who gather for Bible study, praise, and the carrying out of benevolent projects. It is a live organism created and assembled by Christ, governed by His Word, and empowered by His Spirit to complete His Messianic mission. It is God's forever family.

FAMILY RELATIONSHIPS ARE BASED ON LOVE

The principal at our local high school had dealt with one recalcitrant student on repeated occasions. He had exhausted every form of punishment he could devise with no visible results. In desperation he exclaimed, "I have tried everything I know to correct your behavior and nothing has worked. What do you suggest that I do?" I am not sure he expected any response, but I am confident he did not expect the one he received. The young man replied, "Why don't you try love? No one has ever loved me!" Yes, the world is desperately seeking authentic love.

As I read the story of the final Passover meal Jesus shared with His disciples, I can only wonder what impact this event must have had on their lives as they looked back on it after the resurrection. The humbling experience of having their feet washed by the King must have been a constant reminder of their arrogance and His humility. No doubt it fueled their desire to serve the King by serving others.

But later that evening, after the departure of Judas, Jesus gave them a new and final commandment—"A new commandment I give to you, that you love one another, even as I have loved you, that you also love one another. By this all men will know that you are My disciples, if you have love for one another" (Jn. 13:34-35). We know this verse well, but do we follow its dictates? Jesus loved His disciples without reservation. He loved them with a steadfast love. He loved them when they arrogantly desired an exalted place in His coming kingdom. He loved them when they failed Him. Is this love characteristic of the church today? Could the lack of authentic love be one of the reasons the world finds it so easy to ignore the church?

There is no doubt that the early church expressed such love. The picture of the church portrayed in Acts 2:42-47 has long fascinated me. The devotion to fellowship, the willingness to share possessions with those in need, the sheer enjoyment of one another's company as they took meals together "with gladness and sincerity of heart" (2:46), makes me want to belong to such a family of believers. Is there any reason that the modern day church cannot experience and express family love in the same measure and manner as the first century church?

Paul prayed passionately for the churches he founded. He prayed that they would understand who they were in Christ, that they would comprehend the power available to them, and that they might experience the full measure of Christ's love (cf. Eph. 1:18-23 and 3:14-21).

In Ephesians 3:17-18, Paul pays particular attention to the matter of Christ's love. He speaks of the church as being "rooted and grounded in love." Love is its very foundation, its source of stability. Further, he prays that believers will experience Christ's love in its breadth, length, height, and depth. We are impressed today when we can watch a movie in 3-D, but Paul speaks of love in four dimensions. But the most curious phrase occurs when he prays that Christians would "know the love of Christ which surpasses knowledge" (3:19).

How does one know something which surpasses knowledge? The key to this divine riddle is in the phrase "with all the saints" (18). The love of Christ is so vast that none of us can know it alone. Our life experiences are simply too limited. But when we gather as the church, each of us can bear witness to our experience of one small piece of Christ's love. As each member shares his/her experience of Christ's love we assemble a beautiful masterpiece as if we were placing the pieces of a picture puzzle together.

FAMILIES EXPRESS KOINONIA

The Greek word *koinonia* is variously rendered as "association, communion, fellowship, close relationship, generosity, proof of brotherly unity, or gift." In our first look at the early church in Acts 2:42, the word "fellowship" is a rendering of the Greek Word *koinonia*. If you read the entire paragraph, you will see that genuine fellowship always has a practical expression. Too often today, we think of fellowship in terms of a pot-luck dinner or a gathering of a small group for fun and games, but families express fellowship through acts of kindness and generosity that serve as proof of authentic relationships.

True fellowship overcomes artificial barriers.

The church in Antioch, pictured in Acts 11, was the first church planted in a predominately Gentile community. The growth of this church was so spectacular that Barnabas was commissioned by the church in Jerusalem to visit the church. Luke tells us that upon his arrival, he "witnessed the grace of God" (11:23). What did Barnabas see that convinced him that he was seeing sheer grace at work? He saw Jews and Gentiles enjoying genuine fellowship with one another. He saw social, economic, political, cultural, and religious barriers broken down by a power that could only be from God.

It is likely that Paul may have had this church in mind when he wrote Ephesians 2:11-12. In the first verses of Ephesians 2 Paul speaks of the mystery of redemption by which those who were formerly children of wrath became the children of God. Paul then declares that believers are God's workmanship, created for good works. The context suggests that one aspect of being God's workmanship is fellowship which transcends all earthly barriers.

Words such as "separated, excluded, strangers, having no hope, and without God" (2:12) are replaced by "fellow-citizens with the saints, God's household, and a dwelling of God in the Spirit" (2:19, 22). How did such a miracle of transformation and reconciliation occur? "But now in Christ Jesus you who formerly were far off were brought near by the blood of Christ. For He himself is our peace, who made both groups into one and broke down the barrier of the dividing wall… so that in Himself he might make the two into one new man, thus establishing peace" (2:13-15). We speak often about transformation when it comes to church but seldom do we talk of reconciliation. Are there walls of separation in your church that hinder family relationships?

The Nature of Fellowship

In the first seven verses of John's first letter the word fellowship occurs four times. Terms of proclamation literally explode from the page as we read the first three verses. John's desire is to "testify" and "proclaim" about eternal life. His passion for proclamation is driven by his desire that others "may have fellowship with us; and indeed our fellowship is with the Father, and with His Son Jesus Christ" (1 Jn. 1:3). The pathway to true fellowship is the declaration of the Gospel. Evangelism and fellowship are twins. Authentic fellowship can never be diluted by numerical increase. In truth, it is diluted when we lose our passion for sharing with those who do not know the Word of Life.

Notice that the basis of fellowship is our shared relationship with Christ. John tells us that genuine fellowship is human, divine, and joyous (3-4). When a person is saved, he/she not only experiences fellowship with God and His Son, he/she experiences fellowship "with us." Any claim to a vital relationship with God that does not find expression in the human fellowship of other believers is a fraud. When fellowship is expanded through the proclamation of the "Word of Life" joy is made complete (4).

If neither numerical growth nor artificial human barriers can create a barrier to biblical fellowship, what can? The answer is sin—unconfessed and unforgiven sin. "If we say that we have fellowship with Him and yet walk in darkness, we lie and do not practice the truth" (1:6). Think about it for a minute. When there is disunity and broken relationships in your own family, what is the issue? It is sin and our stubborn pride. Our unwillingness to deal with our sin is the problem. The same is true in the church.

How, then, can we heal broken relationships and restore true biblical fellowship? "But if we walk in the Light as He Himself is in the Light, we have fellowship with one another, and the blood of Jesus His Son cleanses us from all sin" (7). Did you notice that sin breaks our fellowship with God and forgiveness restores our fellowship with each other? True forgiveness and restored intimacy with God will be seen in our human relationships. Are there broken relationships in your church family? What are you willing to do to restore them? Before you argue that you are not the one at fault read 1 John 1:8-10.

FAMILIES THRIVE ON UNITY

The church in Corinth was plagued by divisions which made a simple task such as celebrating the Lord's Supper a challenge (1 Cor. 11:18). Paul indicated that the existence of such deep-seated factions was actually evidence that some persons claiming to be part of the church were not actually approved as part of the community. Persons who would persist in disrupting the work and ministry of the church indicate by such behavior that they are not actually believers.

The discussion of the Lord's Supper is followed by the discussion of the ministry of the gifted community. Paul stresses the theme of unity throughout by the repetition of the phrase, "same Spirit" (12:4), "same Lord" (5), and "same God" (6). The variety of gifts and ministries is distributed by the One who expresses unity in His very triune nature.

Paul illustrates this unity by comparing the church to a human body with many members. These members, while varied in function, are nonetheless members of the same body and therefore cannot claim to have no need of the other body parts. In truth, God has constructed the body by sovereign design, providing unity through diversity (12:18).

Paul again is prepared to discuss the function of the gifted body in Ephesians chapter 4. He begins this discussion with the exhortation to behave in a manner worthy of one's calling. This requires humility, gentleness, patience, and tolerance. Such attributes will enable the members to "preserve the unity of the Spirit in the bond of peace." Notice that unity is a gift of the Spirit which requires human response if it is to be preserved. Paul describes the basis of our unity. "There is one body and one Spirit, just as also you were called in one hope of your calling; one Lord, one faith, one baptism, one God and Father of all who is over all and through all and in all" (4:4-6). Unity is the basis for all gifted ministry within the body and thus must be safeguarded with diligence. Do you strive to preserve the unity in your church?

FAMILY MEMBERS ENCOURAGE ONE ANOTHER

Throughout my life, my greatest encouragers have been the members of my family. Now that I am a father and grandfather, I can honestly say that I have no greater joy than seeing family members succeed in life. I want to be an encourager. The book of Hebrews contains both warning and encouragement for believers who were facing the testing of their faith.

In chapter 10 the author reminds believers of the confidence they have to enter the holy place through the blood of Christ. This access was provided by the death of the great high priest. Based on this direct access, Paul challenges believers to three specific activities by the repetition of the phrase "let us." We should draw near in worship, hold fast to our confession, and stimulate one another to love and good deeds—"Not forsaking our own assembling together, as is the habit of some, but encouraging one another; and all the more as you see the day drawing near" (10:25).

Are you fulfilling these three apostolic challenges? Are you part of the problem or the solution?

CONNECTED COMMUNITY
WE ARE HIS BODY

CHAPTER 6

The image of the church as the body of Christ must surely be one of the most intimate pictures imaginable concerning the relationship between Christ and church. It is surpassed only by the image of the church as the bride of Christ. Paul actually links the two in Ephesians 5:28-30, a text often used for teaching on the intimacy of the marriage relationship. Yet, at the very end of the passage, Paul confesses that his primary focus throughout is on Christ and His bride, the church. "This mystery is great; but I am speaking with reference to Christ and the church" (5:32).

So let's take a moment and listen to a declaration of love by the groom for his bride. "So husbands ought also to love their own wives as their own bodies. He who loves his own wife loves himself; for no one ever hated his own flesh, but nourishes and cherishes it, just as Christ also does the church, because we are members of His body" (5:28-30). Christ loves and cherishes His body and we are the members of that body! A stunning and moving thought! Why is the image of the body used to describe the church and what does it mean practically today?

THE BODY DEMANDS UNITY

I can still remember those early teenage years when my body outgrew my coordination. I had the physical size and ability to accomplish certain tasks, but the coordination for the same was lacking. The human body and the church body require unity to enable it to fulfill its potential.

The church at Corinth was rife with dissension. Jealousy and strife were rampant. Factions were claiming to follow Paul, Apollos, Cephas, and Christ (1:12 and 3:4). Sides were being drawn based on the possession of certain spectacular gifts. Disunity was so rampant, the church was having trouble celebrating the Lord's Supper, an event which should have been a source of unity.

Paul's first use of the body metaphor is found in 1 Corinthians 10:16b-17. "Is not the bread we break a sharing in the body of Christ? Since there is one bread, we who are many are one body; for we all partake of the one bread." The central thrust of the image is clear and the word picture is graphic. The loaf, before it is broken into individual pieces is a whole. The church, while made up of many diverse members, is one body precisely because all are incorporated into community by their relationship with Christ.

In chapter 11 where Paul describes the actual celebration of the Lord's Supper, he writes, "For he who eats and drinks, eats and drinks judgment to himself if he does not judge the body rightly" (11:29). The judgment in this case results in earthly punishment (30) and is unlike the judgment discussed in verse 27 which speaks of one who eats in "an unworthy manner" and is therefore guilty of the body and blood of the Lord. The "unworthy manner" of verse 27 means that person has not turned to Christ for redemption.

The reference to "judge the body rightly" recalls the warning of 10:17 which speaks of the failure to appreciate and preserve the unity of the body, which is the church. Thus Paul is warning here about the disunity exhibited in the rich abusing the poor in the celebrating of the Lord's Supper (11:20-22). But the principle is applicable to all issues which are divisive and thus a hindrance to the ministry of the body, which belongs to Christ by redemption. I fear that we accept a lack of unity as the norm. Nothing can be further from the truth and nothing is more detrimental to the life of the believer and the work of the church. We cannot allow our petty differences to impact the unity and ministry of the body of Christ. Too much is at stake for us to play church and wink at sinful disunity. This passage is a somber warning to those who promote or allow disunity to cripple their church.

UNITY THE FOUNDATION FOR EFFECTIVE MINISTRY

In chapter 12 Paul begins his extended discussion of spiritual gifts. It becomes quickly apparent that confusion exists as to the nature and purpose of the gifts. Some in the community are desirous of the more spectacular gifts, apparently claiming them as evidence of their spiritual superiority. Others see themselves as lacking both gifts and purpose in terms of the ministry of the church. These same two issues afflict the church today.

Throughout verses 4-11, Paul stresses the necessity of diversity and unity for the effective ministry of the church. If you read the verses in context, you will find the repetition of the words "varieties" and "same." The variety of gifts, ministries, and effects are accomplished by the one Triune God. All the gifts are given by for the "common good (7) and are given by the same Spirit, "distributing to each one individually just as He wills" (11). At this point Paul employs an extensive use of the body imagery to illustrate the work of the church.

Unity in the church is the work of the Spirit.

"For even as the body is one and yet has many members, and all the members of the body, though they are many, are one body, so also is Christ. For by one Spirit we were all baptized into one body, whether Jews or Greeks, whether slaves or free, and we were all made to drink of one Spirit" (12-13). The conclusion to verse 12 may seem abrupt—"so also is Christ." The jolting nature of the phrase was intended to direct the reader's attention from the human illustration to the spiritual truth. We might have expected Paul to have written—"so also is the church." He employs the more dramatic phrase, "so also is Christ" because the church is not merely an earthly assemblage of many members; it is the body of Christ.

A single human body is composed of different members, such as ears, eyes, hands, etc. The church is a single body composed of the variously gifted members. Its unity is made possible because the many members were baptized by the one Spirit, the act of redemption that placed them into the one body. The moment you were saved, the Spirit immersed you into the body of Christ (13 and cf. Rom. 8:9, 15-17). We express this heavenly reality by developing an intimate relationship with Christ's earthly body, the church.

"Churchless Christianity" and "apathetic membership" are the two most dangerous elements of modern day Christianity. While some persons today claim Christ but ignore the church, many others go through the motion of joining a church but then treat it as if it is nothing more than another organization like a community club or fraternal group. No other earthly institution has the significance of the church. It alone holds the keys to the kingdom (Matt. 16:19) and it alone remains for all eternity (Rev. 21:2). When a "professed believer" ignores the body of Christ or treats it with apathy, it is an egregious sin and a reproach to Christ who sent His Spirit to immerse the redeemed into His body.

Unity does not mean uniformity.

Immediately following his declaration of unity, Paul writes; "For the body is not one member, but many." Christian unity is unique because it preserves and demands individuality. Paul's reference to various national and social groupings—"Jews and Greeks... slaves or free"—reflects the makeup of the church in Corinth.

To further illustrate the necessity of diversity for the unity of the church Paul employs an extended illustration of the working of the human body. Paul's use of a familiar image is striking because the examples often verge on the ridiculous and the humorous as body parts argue with one another. The foot and the ear are first pictured as complaining that they are not part of the body because they are not the hand or the eye. They look and perform differently simply because they have different functions and each is uniquely created for its function. The parts differ because the body demands diversity in function for unity in action.

The arguments among the body parts remind us of an immature child who determines to take his ball and bat and go home because he wasn't chosen to pitch. Tragically, such childish actions are repeated by church members who are offended because they weren't asked to teach a class or sing a solo. Childhood games are childish but not dangerous. When we play such childish games in the church, they are dangerous because they impede the work of the church for the advancing of God's kingdom.

The body is designed by the Creator.

A lack of unity is nothing less than rebellion against the Creator who designed the body. "But now God has placed the members, each one of them, in the body, just as He desired" (12:18). It is for this reason that the various members of the body cannot tell other members they may deem less important that they don't need them. The body is designed by the Master Architect who creates it to accomplish the task for which it is designed.

A mystery exists that will only be resolved when we get to heaven. We often think that we have chosen a church, but behind our choice is the creative process of God who has designed us for His body and placed us in it just as He desires. This means that you are important to the work of the church! It means that you must allow God to show you how He has designed you and gifted you for ministry in His body. If you are still thinking this verse applies to everyone but you, I would point out that the emphatic "each one of them" actually interrupts the flow of the sentence. You have been placed in the body by design and your function is vital to the effective ministry of your church.

When someone arrogantly claims that they can serve the Lord without being a part of the local church, they are ignoring the design and desire of the Creator. We are not independent believers, we are interdependent. We need each other to function properly as the body. There are no useless or insignificant parts in God's design. Paul underlines this truth by reminding his readers—"...it is much truer that the members of the body which seem to be weaker are necessary" (12:22). This language reflects the opinion of the spiritually elite concerning members without impressive spectacular gifts. Such a distorted evaluation of another person's value to the body ignores the truth that "God has so composed the body, giving more abundant honor to that member which lacked, so that there may be no division in the body, but that the members may have the same care for one another" (12:24b-25).

The design of the body mandates mutual care.

When each member discovers his/her role and functions according to God's design, there will be harmonious relationships, mutual care (25) and total empathy (26). We have already seen an example where mutual care was conspicuously lacking in Corinth. When they took the Lord's Supper, the wealthy came early and ate to excess while the poor left hungry. This lack of concern was not only shaming the poor; it was despising the church of God (11:21-22).

Now in chapter 12 Paul takes the matter of mutual care a step further. As members of the same body, we are so closely bound together that we share the same feelings. What causes joy to one member delights the whole body and, conversely, when one member suffers the entire body hurts. We can illustrate this truth from the human body. We stump our toe and find that our altered gait soon leads to a sore back which affects the whole body. Paul underlines once more the vital truth—"Now you are Christ's body, and individually members of it" (12:27). The body imagery was being applied specifically to the church at Corinth, but its principles are applicable to every church of every generation.

THE BODY IS EMPOWERED TO EXPRESS GOD'S FULLNESS

Colossians and Ephesians were written later in Paul's ministry. The churches in pro-Consular Asia were being threatened by false doctrine. According to these foreign ideas the *pleroma* (fullness), an impersonal divine force, exploded and sparks of divinity now reside in all of us. Various cosmic powers, emanations of divinity, can assist people in their contact with God and therefore people need to supplement their reliance on Christ by an acquaintance with such powers. Sounds very similar to current "new age" teaching, doesn't it?

Paul attacks this heretical teaching directly in Colossians 1 where he declares that all created things owe their existence to Christ (1:16) who has triumphed over all heavenly powers (1:20). Christ is not to be compared with any cosmic power as if He was nothing more than one emanation of the divinity among others. Paul declares that it was the Father's pleasure for all the *pleroma* (fullness) to dwell in Christ. We are not searching for enlightenment so we can contact the impersonal divine force. We are redeemed by the One who is the *pleroma* of God.

As such Christ is head over everything, which includes His church (*ecclesia*). "He is also head of the body the church; and He is the beginning, the firstborn from the dead, so that He Himself will come to have first place in everything" (1:18). Paul repeats this idea of the body three more times in Colossians. In 1:24 he speaks with awe of his privilege of being a minster of this church. In chapter 2:19 he speaks of Christ as head of the church from whom the whole body is supplied with nourishment which enables it to grow with a growth which is from God. In 3:14-15 he calls them to put on love, live in unity, and to allow the peace of Christ to rule in them since they were called in one body.

In Ephesians, the companion letter, Paul applies the word "fullness" to the church in a bold and demanding way. We would readily agree that Jesus was the "fullness" of God. But would you be willing to apply that same word to the church? Paul does! In chapter one Paul prays that believers would understand the hope of God's calling, the riches of His inheritance in the saints, and the surpassing power available to those who believe (1:18-19). He then speaks of the power of the resurrection and exaltation of Christ which placed Him above all rule authority and power. Now listen carefully—"And He put all things in subjection under His feet, and gave Him as head over all things to the church, which is His body, the fullness of Him who fills all in all" (1:22-23).

The church, the earthly body of Christ, is empowered to express God's *pleroma* (fullness) in the same manner that Christ did during His incarnation. In chapter 3:8-10 Paul writes of the privilege which was his to unveil a mystery hidden for ages by God who created everything. That mystery was God's plan to make His manifold wisdom known though the church and He carried out this eternal purpose by sending Christ. He came to establish the church and His Messianic ministry will be completed by the church.

In chapter 3 Paul again breaks into impassioned prayer for the church. He prays that believers might be strengthened with power through the Spirit, experience the indwelling Christ, and be able to comprehend "with all the saints" the love of Christ so that "you may be filled up to all the fullness of God" (3:19). This may sound like a tall order, but not for the church. God is able to do more than we ask or think "according to the power that works within us." How does God accomplish His work on earth now that Jesus sits at His right hand? His power works within us—the church. It is for that reason that God receives glory in the church and in Christ Jesus for all generations.

Is it possible for the church to express God's fullness even as Christ did? It is not only possible, it is imperative. In chapter four Paul gives the practical formula that enables the church to express God's fullness. He first calls believers to walk worthy of their calling (1) and then to express the unity which is provided by the Spirit (2-6). Once again Paul speaks of the unique gifting of the church accomplished by the exaltation of Christ (7-10). One aspect of this gifting was leaders who equip the gifted member to accomplish the work of service "until we all attain to the unity of the faith, and of the knowledge of the Son of God, to a mature man, to the measure of the stature which belongs to the fullness of Christ" (4:13).

Does your church express God's fullness? If not, why not? Are you part of the problem or the solution?

CONNECTED COMMUNITY
ME, A PRIEST?

CHAPTER 7

Did you know that you are called to be part of a community empowered to serve as priests, offering up spiritual sacrifices acceptable to God? Did I catch you off guard? Persons who have grown up in the evangelical tradition rarely think about priests and their work. We think more of pastors, deacons, and elders and regard "priests" as part of the high church tradition. Yet, the priesthood of believers is a beautiful designation for the members of the body of Christ.

Here's how Peter speaks of members of the body of Christ. "You also, as living stones, are being built up as a spiritual house for a holy priesthood, to offer up spiritual sacrifices acceptable to God through Jesus Christ… but you are A CHOSEN RACE, A royal PRIESTHOOD, A HOLY NATION, A PEOPLE FOR God's OWN POSSESSION, so that you may proclaim the excellencies of Him who has called you out of darkness into His marvelous light" (1 Peter 2:5, 9). Peter uses several Old Testament images that are intricately intertwined to speak of the privilege and responsibility for ministry in and through the church, the body of Christ.

The first image is that of a temple which is made up of living stones, which testifies to the vital growing nature of the New Testament church. The church is designed and commissioned to grow as it embraces the task of expanding the kingdom by fulfilling the

Great Commission. "Holy priesthood" underlines the ministry of believers who are called to offer up spiritual sacrifices. "Chosen Race," "Holy Nation," and "God's Possession" speak of the believers' privilege of representing a Holy God to a fallen world so they too might worship their rightful King.

LIVING STONES IN A HOLY TEMPLE

The essential image of this entire section is that of a spiritual house or temple where acceptable sacrifices are offered up to God through Christ. This idea is reminiscent and consistent with Paul's teaching that believers are the present-day temple of God—the place of worship and service. Remember his question to the Corinthians—"Do you not know that you are a temple of God and that the Spirit of God dwells in you?" (1 Cor. 3:16).

In 1 Peter the church is viewed as a spiritual house which is made alive and growing by the presence and power of Christ. The growth of the building is supernaturally empowered but it is power which is made available to the church through the living stones. The unique linking of sovereign activity and human response is a consistent teaching of Scripture. The active participation of "living stones" is crucial to divine activity on earth.

When we take the image of "living stones" seriously, we see ourselves as stones integrally joined with those of the great men and women of every age who have placed their life at God's disposal and are thus living stones in God's earthly temple. Can you imagine a stone with your name on it placed beside one with the name of King David, Paul, Charles Spurgeon, or Billy Graham? In case you missed it, the corner stone of this building was Christ Himself (1 Pt. 2:6-7). His position was purchased by His death and made possible our inclusion in this holy temple. Nothing should humble, challenge, or thrill us more than the thought that God has allowed us to be a living stones in His holy temple. It calls us to give our all in service and praise to Him.

A HOLY PRIESTHOOD

The picture now shifts slightly as if we are viewing a beautiful diamond from a different perspective. Believers who were first pictured as stones in the building are now seen as priests serving within the temple. Since the temple exists exclusively for the service of God, it must be populated by a holy people who offer up acceptable sacrifices to Him.

The image of a priestly people for service to a Holy God is first found in Exodus 19:5-6. "Now then, if you will indeed obey My voice and keep My covenant, then you shall be My own possession among all the peoples, for all the earth is Mine; and you shall be to Me a kingdom of priests and a holy nation." Notice that before Israel can serve as a priestly people they must respond to the call to radical obedience and holiness. The God who they represent is Holy.

If you take a moment to read 1 Peter 1:13-22, you will discover that the call to radical obedience and the resulting holiness is the foundation for our priestly service. The call to sacrificial service is based on the precious nature of our redemption, which was purchased by the blood of Christ (19). Our obedience to the truth purified our souls for a sincere love of the brethren (22). Our priestly service is not our singular duty but a corporate responsibility. The priesthood of the believers is a corporate concept and therefore once again we are called to intimate community relationships.

Since we are called to serve as priests, we must understand the functions of a priestly people. We find a vital clue in chapter 2, verse 5—"to offer up spiritual sacrifices." The idea of a priest devoid of an accompanying sacrifice is incongruous. The word "spiritual" indicates that our sacrifices are of a different nature than the animal sacrifices of the Old Testament.

In truth, the Old Testament paved the way for the understanding of spiritual sacrifices. The Psalmist spoke of a sacrifice of thanksgiving (Ps. 50:13-14). In Psalm 141:2, prayer is viewed as an incense offering. The prophet Micah declares that God is not delighted with thousands of rams and rivers of oil, but desires rather justice, love, kindness, and a humble walk with one's God (6:7-8).

Let's look together at five sacrifices required of a priestly people.

Our physical bodies. The most basic sacrifice we are required to offer God is our own bodies. "I urge you therefore, brethren, by the mercies of God to present your bodies a living and holy sacrifice, acceptable to God, which is your spiritual service of worship" (Rom. 12:1). We have nothing more to give God than our physical bodies. He wants nothing more and nothing less. The good news is that He has already declared this gift "acceptable." What you have to offer is well pleasing to Him. When you read the remainder of Romans 12, you will discover that the ensuing discussion relates to spiritual gifts. Your gifts reside in your physical body and thus when you present yourself to God you are putting your abilities for service at his disposal.

Our unique ministry. In Romans 15:16, Paul writes of his ministry to the Gentiles as an offering sanctified by the Spirit. First, we should note that Gentiles were the result of Paul's ministry in evangelism and church planting. Every believer is called and equipped to bear witness to the gospel and one day it will be our privilege to place other lives on the altar as our acceptable sacrifice to the risen King. Like Paul, every believer is called to a unique ministry either in or through the church. What ministry are you prepared to lay before the King?

Our good deeds. "Do not neglect doing good and sharing; for with such sacrifices God is pleased" (Heb. 13:16). Good deeds are not the means of redemption, but they are always the result of redemption (James 2:18-26). Every believer will be judged for their works in this body (Rev. 20:12). Can you imagine the excitement of laying all your good deeds as an acceptable offering?

Our worship. Worship is both a privilege and an offering of an acceptable sacrifice. "Through Him then let us continually offer up a sacrifice to God, that is, the fruit of lips that give thanks to His name" (Heb. 13:15). We cannot claim to be functioning as priests unless we are regularly offering up the sacrifice of praise through our attendance and full participation in the worship activities of our local church. But worship is not to be confined to an hour or two on Sunday morning; it is the constant giving of ourselves to the King as an act of worship that God desires. In Romans 12:1 Paul speaks of the offering of ourselves as a "spiritual service of worship."

Our stewardship. Paul, in thanking the Philippians for their financial support of his ministry, called their offering "a fragrant aroma, an acceptable sacrifice, well-pleasing to God" (Phil. 4:18). The writer to the Hebrews includes "sharing" along with "doing good" as sacrifices which please God (13:16). We sometimes treat the time of offering as if it is an intrusion in the service of worship. When we place His tithe and our offerings in the plate we need to see it as a priestly privilege and an act of consecrated worship that we are laying before the King.

Have you noticed that the emphasis throughout is on the *duties* of priesthood rather than on *status* or *privilege*? It is indeed an exhilarating privilege to serve the King of kings as a priestly people, but it is the service of a priestly people which seems to be missing today. According to most studies, only about 20% of those people who claim to be part of this priestly community ever contribute in any meaningful way in the mission or ministry of their local church family. Why the disconnect?

A PEOPLE FOR GOD'S OWN POSSESSION

Just listen to these declarations—"You are a chosen race, a royal priesthood, a holy nation, a people for

God's own possession" (1 Pt. 2:9). The emphasis is on our *corporate* identity. I do not function as a priest in isolation but only as part of the redeemed people of God. The biblical references to the priesthood of believers are plural, a point underlined by the use of phrases such as "kingdom of priests" or "royal priesthood." May I reiterate, the New Testament does not recognize the "Lone Ranger" concept of Christianity which is gaining in popularity. Nor does it endorse the apathetic spectator style of membership practiced by a growing segment of the church.

We are corporately God's people because He purchased us by the sacrifice of His only Son. Now He desires to fully indwell us. "Why," you might ask, "does God desire to inhabit a people?" The text is crystal clear on this matter—"that you may proclaim the excellencies of Him who has called you out of darkness into His marvelous light" (9). Our lives and our words must be such that they reveal the true nature of the Light to those who live in great darkness. Peter once again underlines the call to holy living so that our very behavior, our good deeds, would cause the nations to "glorify God in the day of visitation" (12).

God has chosen to reveal Himself on earth through His priestly people. He has chosen to accomplish all kingdom activity through a people that He fully indwells. Does this sound like your church? Are you part of the problem or part of the solution?

GIFTED FOR PRIESTLY SERVICE

You may be thinking that you are not *worthy* or *capable* of serving as a priest. I have great news for you.

You have been made *worthy* by the sacrificial death of Christ and you have been made *capable* by the gifting of the Spirit. The clear teaching of the Bible is that *you are created in God's image, redeemed by His grace, gifted and empowered by His Spirit, and placed in His body by design*. We were created and redeemed for good works "which God prepared beforehand so that we would walk in them" (Eph. 2:10).

If you are concerned that you have never found yourself on any of the gift lists in the New Testament, you can relax. Those lists differ because Paul was using them as illustrations as the sort of activities that God can empower believers to accomplish in and through His church. They are not intended to be comprehensive.

Paul provides a simple overview of his teaching on spiritual gifts in Romans 12:1-8. Paul establishes first the foundation for understanding and using our gifts for the King. We must present ourselves to God for service. God is interested in *availability* not *ability*. Our "assumed" weakness is the platform for the display of God's power. Second, we are to live by the transformation of our mind. We must see ourselves from God's perspective—redeemed, empowered, and gifted. When we take these two spiritual steps it enables us to know and do the will of God for our lives which God has already deemed, "good, acceptable, and perfect."

Here are five things you should know about gifts:

The principle of sound judgment. Paul insists that believers should not think too highly of themselves, but to think with sound judgment. There are two dangers with spiritual gifts. Some people seek them and see them as badges of spiritual attainment. This leads to spiritual arrogance. Some see themselves as lacking gifts. This leads to spiritual apathy. Both are wrong and both hurt the work of the body. The gifts of grace (*charismata*) tell us nothing about the possessor, only the giver.

The principle of universal giftedness. The phrase, "Since we have gifts" (12:6) is the basic teaching behind the entire passage. In 1 Corinthians 12:6-7 Paul speaks of "all" and "each" as being gifted. You are not designed to be a spectator in the body of Christ. You were uniquely created and gifted by God for a special role that will enable you to advance His kingdom on earth and thus live with eternal impact.

The principle of unity through diversity. "For just as we have many members in one body and all the members do not have the same function, so we, who are many are one body in Christ" (Rom. 12:4-5a). In 1 Corinthians 12 Paul employs a somewhat humorous argument among body members about the relative importance of the various members of the body to establish that God has placed each of the gifted members in the body by His design.

The principle of interdependence. The phrase "individually members one of another" (Rom. 12:5b) breaks the parallelism with verse 4 and thus stands out in bold relief. Gifts should never lead to arrogant isolation; for they actually cause us to be interdependent. When a gifted member severs himself from the life of the body, he becomes useless for kingdom activity.

The principle of the common good. Gifts are not given for our amusement nor the amazement of our friends. They are given for the common good of the body.

Here are a few wonderful truths I want you to act upon. You are gifted to participate in God's kingdom activity. You have been chosen to be God's co-laborer. You are important to God's work through His church. The task God has created and gifted you to accomplish is significant because God has deemed it so.[1]

---

1   If you want to understand more about spiritual gifts and how to discover and deploy your gift(s), *You Are Gifted* book, study guide and DVD would be a good follow up study.

CONNECTED COMMUNITY
STRUCTURED FOR EFFECTIVENESS

Every living and healthy organism and organization must have structure to survive and thrive. There must be a clearly understood process for making decisions and implementing strategy. Every church needs a clearly defined structure that will enable it to accomplish its God-given purpose. Often churches develop their own informal, but clearly understood structure, based on community status or church tradition without any real attention to God's design. Since God sent His only Son to establish the church, provided His Holy Spirit to empower the church, and placed the members in it as He desired, we should first ask whether there is a God-given pattern for church structure.

As we investigate the New Testament, we will find several consistent themes. First, every member ministry is the norm and thus the Spirit gifts each member for unique service. Second, some persons are gifted for leadership roles and must be loved and respected for the sake of the mission of the church. Third, the entire congregation is involved in the larger decision making process. These truths must be affirmed and practiced in the context of love which demands that we place the needs of others above our own and the mission of the church above all else.

THE NEED FOR LEADERS

I love reading the book of Acts and I often find it hard to get beyond chapter two. I am thrilled to think of an ingathering baptismal service which involved three thousand or more persons (2:41). Words like "continually," "devoted," and "together" speak of a passion and an intimacy that is largely missing in churches today. The early church was a community of Spirit-filled people who turned the world upside down. Its rapid growth created challenges which became opportunities to see God at work in the "seemingly" mundane.

The Congregation Elects Deacons

Acts 6 begins with a simple statement of fact—"Now at this time while the disciples were increasing in number, a complaint arose…." Notice two things. Growth is the norm for the Spirit-empowered church. Second, growth creates challenges. Too often, when churches experience growth and the accompanying challenges, they settle into a "let's-not-rock-the-boat" mentality rather than looking for God's provision.

The particular challenge in this instance was the ability of the "twelve" to provide for the needs of the widows and, at the same time, focus on the ministry of the Word (2). The apostles explained the issue to the congregation of believers and suggested that they select qualified men (3) for this unique and necessary ministry to enable the apostles to continue to accomplish their ministry of leading the church in prayer and the ministry of the word (5). The idea was looked upon favorably by the entire congregation (6) and the first "deacons" were elected.

The English word "deacon" comes from the word translated "serve tables" (*diakonos*). It seems clear that deacons were to handle the practical tasks of the church especially involving the care of the physical needs of church members. Tragically many churches have established "deacon boards" that have understood their role as that of leading or administrating the affairs of the church rather than serving the needs of the people. Deacons have become more involved in the business of the church and have thus missed the blessing of accomplishing the ministry task God gave them.

In many instances this has left the God-ordained and church-called pastor with little voice in the establishing of vision and administrative oversight of the direction of the church. It has led to an unbiblical and ineffective conclusion that the pastor is responsible for the entire weight of the pastoral care of the flock. This, in turn, has led to massive pastoral burn-out and inefficiency in fulfilling the Great Commission.

The serving of the widows was not a menial task, below the dignity of the apostles. The meeting of these practical needs was critical to the ongoing effectiveness of the church. It was simply not the task which God had called the apostles to fulfill. Therefore a new opportunity for servant leadership emerged in the providence of God. There are no menial tasks in the New Testament church and there are no insignificant members. A quick glance at the rigorous qualifications required of those who would serve as deacons (1 Tim. 3:8-13) will demonstrate their importance to the health of the growing church.

A Pattern Established

The church at Jerusalem is a bit unique since it was led by the twelve apostles. For that reason, it is important for us to look at the pattern established as new churches were planted by the early missionaries. Acts 14 provides us with fifty-yard-line seats for watching Paul and Barnabas at work.

Paul and Barnabas complete their first tumultuous missionary journey in Derbe, having made many disciples (14:21). In spite of the persecution they had faced in the first half of their journey, they courageously return to Antioch by way of Lystra and Iconium. Their goal was to strengthen the new believers by encouraging them to continue in the faith. Further, they warned them to expect persecution and tribulation. They spared no punches as they made it clear that following Jesus was not for the faint at heart.

Their long term strategy, however, was to establish leaders in each community. "When they had appointed elders for them in every church, having prayed with fasting, they commended them to the Lord in whom they had believed" (14:23). These church planters knew that without leaders to teach and encourage the believers, the church would not thrive nor long survive.

The use of the term "elder" (*presbuteros*) was based on the Jewish model of elders who served in local synagogues. At this early state the church was more concerned with structure and function than they were with titles and positions. The issue then and now is about biblical leadership and not about office or authority.

A PICTURE OF THE EARLY CHURCH LEADERS

Galatians 6:1-6 and I Thessalonians 5:12-14 provide two of the earliest pictures of leadership in the Pauline churches. As we study these passages, we will again find two consistent themes. Every member is responsible for ministry and yet some are called to exercise leadership functions. We should see these as complementary and not competitive ideas. God has ordained leadership structure in the church for the mutual benefit of all the members and the effective expansion of the kingdom through the church.

Galatians 6 is a more abbreviated passage and focuses first on restoration of a fallen brother, bearing one another's burdens, and each person sharing equally in ministry (1-5). In verse 6 Paul indicates that the one who receives teaching should share with the one who provides the teaching. The context suggests that there were persons responsible for the instruction of the congregation who were compensated by the others for that work.

Paul gives us greater detail about the responsibility of the early leaders in 1 Thessalonians 5:12-14. "But we request of you, brethren, that you appreciate those who diligently labor among you, and have charge over you in the Lord and give you instruction, and that you esteem them very highly in love because of their work. Live in peace with one another." Paul outlines three primary tasks for the pastoral leaders of the church.

Leadership Requires Harmonious Relationships

Paul begins by requesting that church members "appreciate" and "esteem highly in love" those whom

God has gifted for leadership. Very little can be accomplished when relationships between members and leaders are strained, fragile, or hostile. Notice that this appeal is not based on personality or personal preferences, but on "their work." When dealing with personality conflicts and personal preferences, we need to remind ourselves of the critical nature of our mission and the important role of God-appointed leaders.

How many times have you seen the mission of your church impaired because of dissension between laity and the leaders? All too often we nurture suspicious attitudes that manifest themselves in a "we/them" mentality. We reflect this attitude with biting humor that hurts both the individual leader and the ministry of the church. For the sake of the kingdom, we must determine that we will do whatever it takes to live in peace with one another.

Three Key Functions for Pastoral Leaders

Three main tasks are described in this passage. These certainly are not a comprehensive description of the work of the pastor; nevertheless, they are central to the effective pastor's work. The Greek structure has three present participles governed by a single article, which suggests that Paul is describing one group of person who perform the three specified tasks.

1. "Labor among" speaks first of the rigorous labor which is involved in pastoral leadership and second to the pastoral care ministry essential to effective leadership. When Paul writes young Timothy, he speaks both of the physical and spiritual fitness required of those called to the

pastorate. I am the son of a pastor and a pastor by calling and I can give personal testimony to the rigorous demands of pastoral ministry. I have been blessed to have members who have appreciated the rigorous demands of pastoral leadership and have given me support and encouragement. I challenge you to be an encourager for your pastor. The word "among" is important because it indicates that pastoral care, by its very nature, is "up close and personal." Laboring among allows the pastor to model and mentor the ministry that must be shared by all members of the body.

2. "Have charge over" indicates that the pastor is called to exercise leadership, oversight, and protection for the congregation. In the Pastoral Epistles, Paul uses the same Greek word to speak of the "overseers" and "deacons" ability to "manage" their own household (I Tim. 3:4, 5 and 12). Those who would lead the church must first prove themselves capable of leading in their own home. In 1 Timothy 5:17 the same word is again used for the "elders" who are good "leaders." Those elders who work hard at their preaching and teaching are worthy of an ample honorarium. Numerous studies have documented that healthy churches entrust their pastor with the responsibility and freedom to oversee the mission of the church. Perhaps you notice that "have charge over" is modified by "in the Lord." Administrative leadership is a spiritual authority given by God and earned through effective service. The pastor is both leader and servant; requiring him to be both powerful and

humble. Surely this attitude is modeled by our Lord who stooped to wash feet and yet clearly led His disciples. We should heed the writer of Hebrews advice—"Obey your leaders and submit to them for they keep watch over your souls as those who will give an account. Let them do this with joy and not with grief, for this would be unprofitable for you" (13:17). Pastors must remember that they will give account to the King for shepherding His flock. Members should note that we will be held accountable for whether we made the task a joy or grief.

3. "Give you instruction" underlines the primary task of doctrinal instruction with the goal of making disciples. When the growth of the church in Jerusalem created a challenge for the apostles, deacons were elected enabling the apostles to devote themselves to the ministry of prayer and preaching. One requirement for the pastor that is not included in those of the deacon is the ability to teach (1 Tim. 3:2). In Ephesians 4:11-16 Paul provides the vital link between those gifted to lead and the membership which is gifted to serve. The pastor/teacher is to equip the saints for the work of ministry. The end result of this shared ministry will be maturity, doctrinal stability and the growth of the body in love.

The question of the titles and number of church leaders is somewhat controversial. Different churches and different denominations use different titles for those in leadership. We are probably more interested in titles than were the members of the early church. They were more interested in *function* rather than *title*, *office*, or *status*. It is likely that we have created titles from words that were simply descriptive of functions.

Three primary terms are found consistently in the New Testament church. The word *elder* translates the Greek *presbuteros*. *Pastor* translates *poimen*, and *overseer* translates *episkopos*. The word elder comes from the synagogue and may have been more commonly used to designate pastoral leaders in churches which were predominately Jewish. The three terms above are often used interchangeably and even in a single context referring to the same persons. In Acts 20:17 Paul called the elders from Ephesus to meet him at Miletus. He exhorts the elders to shepherd the flock over whom God has appointed them overseers. All three Greek terms are used to describe a single group of leaders. You will again find the use of all three terms in 1 Peter 5:2 to speak of one group of persons.

My own best reading is that the three terms are descriptive of the work of the pastor who is then joined in his work by deacons who assist with pastoral care. But rather than split hairs over titles, we simply need to embrace a leadership model that is productive and biblical. We must all put our egos on hold for the sake of the Kingdom.

GOVERNED BY THE SPIRIT

The final decisions on matters concerning the operation of the church are determined by the Holy Spirit and are confirmed by the congregation at large, and not by any small group within the congregation.

The first example of a church-wide action is found in Acts 6 where the twelve "summoned the congregation of disciples" and told them of the challenge facing the church in the feeding of the widows. You can sense the unanimous spirit— "The statement found approval with the whole congregation" (6:5). The congregation proceeds to choose seven men for this task. On another occasion the church at Antioch determined to send Barnabas and Saul for mission service. "Then when they had fasted and prayed and laid hand on them, they sent them away" (13:3). Notice the unanimous spirit and the dependence on prayer.

The Pauline letters presume that there was an opportunity for the whole congregation to hear and respond to Paul's instructions. In 1 Corinthians 5:4-5 he instructs the assembled congregation to discipline a member who had fallen into grave sin. In 2 Corinthians 2:6-7 he speaks of the punishment agreed upon "by the majority" and then indicates that the Corinthians are to forgive and comfort the man who has repented. When the offering that Paul instructs them to collect in 1 Corinthians 16:1-4 is ready for delivery, Paul mentions that Titus and two other trustworthy brothers have been "appointed by the churches" to travel with Paul to Jerusalem (2 Cor. 8:19).

Whatever a church chooses to call its congregational meeting, each church must establish and preserve a shared interest and involvement in major church decisions. The involvement of the congregation in confirming the leadership of the Holy Spirit does not negate the need for strong pastoral leadership, but rather should confirm it. The organizational structure of the church should allow the Spirit to communicate with the entire body of believers thus creating unity of purpose. Any such gathering should focus on prayer not political persuasion. The desire of the congregation is to determine the will of God, not to assert the rights or preferences of any one group.

The single desire of church leaders and church members is to discern the will of God which will enable the body to more effectively fulfill the Great Commission.

CONNECTED COMMUNITY
DISCIPLINED FOR GOD'S GLORY

The late John Stott wrote: "The secular world is almost wholly unimpressed by the church today. There is widespread departure from Christian moral standards. So long as the church tolerates sin in itself and does not judge itself…and fails to manifest visibly the power of Jesus Christ to save from sin, it will never attract the world to Christ."[1]

That statement was published in 1974 but its truth and relevance remains. Research indicates that the lifestyle of many Christians does not differ substantially from that of their unsaved neighbors. The influence and evangelistic effectiveness of the church continues to decline. The public attitude toward the church ranges from apathy to hostility. Are these findings all related? Are our internal problems and our failure to deal with them a part of the reason for our lack of effectiveness? Is the church willing to discipline its members for the sake of God's glory and the church's mission?

We generally do not see discipline in a positive light. We think of it in terms of punishment and our flesh rebels against it. Yet the writer of Hebrews teaches us that discipline is a sign of the Lord's love for His children (12:6), and that those who are not disciplined are not sons, but illegitimate children (8). God's discipline is for our good, "so that we may share

His holiness" (10), and while this discipline may seem sorrowful in the moment it will lead to "peaceful fruit of righteousness." When we view discipline through the prism of God's infinite love, it will be seen as a vital part of our spiritual growth.

Church discipline should never be practiced in the legalistic sense of "kicking people out of the church." Its goal is always the restoration of the brother and its focus is on the manifestation of God's glory through the church. Its practice should always have in mind the mission of the church. Too much is at stake for us to allow serious unrepentant sin to impact the purity and effectiveness of the church.

GOD'S PLAN TO REVEAL HIS CHARACTER THROUGH HIS PEOPLE

Exodus 19:5-6 is a key passage for understanding God's purpose in the calling of Israel to be His own possession. Israel has been redeemed from Egyptian bondage. They now belong to God in a twofold sense—they are His by creation and by redemption. In this passage, we find the people of God camped before the Lord at Mount Sinai while Moses goes up the mountain to hear from God.

God instructs Moses to tell the people; "Now then, if you will indeed obey My voice and keep My covenant, then you shall be My own possession among all the peoples, for all the earth is Mine; and you shall be to Me a kingdom of priests and a holy nation" (5-6a). God's people are called to radical obedience and visible holiness because they have been chosen to represent God on earth in a priestly fashion. God's intention is to empower Israel to join Him in the reclaiming of the peoples of the earth—"for all the earth is Mine."

Israel, however, treats their calling as privilege devoid of responsibility and falls into gross sin. God instructs Ezekiel to tell Israel they are being disciplined because they profaned God's holy name when He sent them among the nations. God's desire is to restore His people to holiness by putting His Spirit within them, enabling them to obey His Word and thus reflect His character once again. The prophet gives us a clear insight of the impact of the restoration of Israel's holiness. "Then the nations will know that I am the Lord," 'declares the Lord God,' "when I prove Myself holy among you in their sight" (36:23). In the remainder of chapter 36, you will find eight different occasions where God promises a positive response from the nations when Israel returns to God and reflects His holiness.

In the New Testament, the church is the community through which God has chosen to reveal Himself and advance His kingdom. In the Ephesian letter, Paul declares that God has placed all things in subjection under Christ's feet for His body, the church. The resurrection and exaltation of Christ empowers the church to express "the fullness of Him who fills all in all" (1:23).

The word translated "fullness" is used in Col. 1:19 and 2:9 to describe Christ as the fullness of God. When we link Colossians 1:19 and Ephesians 1:23, we see that God's ultimate design and desire is to make known

His manifold wisdom to the rulers and authorities in the heavenly places through His church (Eph. 3:10). Discipline is one of the means that God uses to purify His church, enabling it to reflect His character (His fullness) faithfully so that it might be effective in the reaching of the nations.

THE REASONS FOR CHURCH DISCIPLINE

Let's look first at the reasons for church discipline. First, discipline is necessary because it enables the church to more clearly reflect God's glory and thus manifest His character to the world. God has ultimate concern for His glory among the nations. God's holiness is made manifest in the holiness of His people. When we turn a blind eye to continual and unrepentant sin in the church, it reflects on our Father's name. We can't pray, "Hallowed be Your name" and allow sin to be unchecked. Purity is more than a milestone on the way to reconciliation of a sinful church member; it is the calling of God's people.

Second, discipline is critical to the effective fulfillment of our mission. The church received its marching orders from the resurrected Lord. We are called and empowered to disciple the nations (Matt. 28:19-20). Unconfessed and unrepentant sin will negatively impact the church's effectiveness when it comes to the reaching of their community and the world and thus must be dealt with in a compassionate and biblical manner.

Third, discipline has as its ultimate goal the restoration of the fallen one. Matthew 18 is a key text in the understanding of biblical church discipline. We will look at the steps prescribed by our Lord later, but notice that the desired goal is to win one's brother (15). Simply put, the goal of all discipline is repentance and restoration. For this reason, the church must follow the biblical guidelines in a spirit of humility and gentleness when it practices church discipline. In Galatians 6:1 Paul indicates that when a brother is caught in a trespass he should be restored in a spirit of gentleness. Church discipline will never manifest a "holier than you" attitude since believers are aware of their own potential weaknesses (Gal. 6:2).

Fourth, church discipline is a key to maintaining unity in the body of Christ. We have become so accustomed to the lack of unity in the church that we think It is the norm. Unity of the body is the work of the Spirit and the basis for effective gifted service. Therefore we must be "diligent to preserve the unity of the Spirit in the bond of peace" (Eph. 4:3). Sin always has a corporate effect and thus it compromises the unity of the body. In 1 Corinthians 5:6, a passage about church discipline, Paul warns the Corinthians, "Do you not know that a little leaven leavens the whole lump of dough?" When a member of the church sins, it is not an isolated matter; it impacts the entire family. Sin destroys! It mangles! It disrupts fellowship! It weakens resistance! It dulls the conscience and debases the spiritual appetite!

I was in my office preparing for a church council meeting when one of our leaders appeared at my door. It was apparent that he was troubled. Our brief conversation revealed that he had received a ticket for driving under the influence the night before. He had once had a drinking problem but had been sober for years since becoming a Christian. He had just received a promotion at work and, at the encouragement of several friends, had stopped at a bar for "one drink" to celebrate.

He was concerned for how his sin would impact the church and what he should do. We settled on a plan for discipline and restoration. He confessed his sin to his fellow-council members and resigned from his position of leadership. After a time of prayer for restoration, he was warmly embraced and encouraged by others in the room. A time of restoration was decided upon and a means of accountability was established. The unity and ministry of the church was protected and, in due time, this man was restored to effective ministry. When we value both the unity of the church and the spiritual vitality of the individual we will understand the importance of church discipline.

Fifth, we must embrace church discipline because it is biblical. Church discipline is simply an issue of obedience for the church. In Matthew 18, two chapters after Jesus announcement that He intends to build His church, He gives instructions for dealing with the sin both personally and corporately (15-19). In 1 Corinthians 5 we see a vivid example of church discipline prescribed by the Apostle Paul. In 1 Corinthians 6:1-8 Paul assures his readers that they are competent to judge the small matters that occur between brothers since one day they will judge the angels. When the church fails to resolve internal issues through church discipline, it is a defeat for the church.

In 2 Thessalonians chapter 3, Paul instructs the

church on how to deal with brothers who are living an unruly life (6). These persons are leading undisciplined lives, not working at all, and acting like busybodies (11). First, Paul commands the unruly persons to work in a quiet fashion and eat their own bread. However, he indicates that if anyone does not follow instructions, the church is to take special note of them and withdraw fellowship. The desire is that the individual will be put to shame and thus come to repentance (14). The church does treat the individual as an enemy, but admonishes him as a brother (15).

THE CONTEXT AND ATTITUDE FOR DISCIPLINE

Discipline is a family matter and thus the context is always the church as loving family. Texts that we have already considered such as Matthew 18:15-18, 1 Corinthians 5-6 and 2 Thessalonians 3 make it clear that the church is the appropriate context for church discipline. Sin disrupts the fellowship and impacts the unity and ministry of the church and thus this is the only appropriate venue for constructive and restorative discipline. When thinking about the impact and value of church discipline, do not overlook the role of the Holy Spirit in both the conviction of sin and the restoration of the believer. Only the church has the necessary resources to bring constructive discipline.

The attitude is one of humility that seeks first the loving restoration of a fellow member. No one should ever desire to embarrass a family member who is already struggling with an issue of sin. Church discipline is not an opportunity to "get even." We must bear in mind that we are privileged to participate with

God in the healing and restoration of a member of our own body.

THE STEPS OF BIBLICAL DISCIPLINE

The first two steps prescribed by our Lord in Matthew 18 should enable believers to privately resolve most issues and thus enable us to avoid the final step which may require that an individual be placed outside the fellowship and the spiritual protection of the church.

Step 1. "If your brother sins, go and show him his fault in private: if he listens to you, you have won your brother" (Matt. 18:15). First, we are to go alone seeking restoration. Look at the beauty of this first step. If practiced faithfully and prayerfully, it avoids the possibility of gossip and scandal. Tragically, we often tell others about an offense before we actually confront the individual. The word then spreads and people choose sides and the chasm opens wider. Often you will find that the whole issue was based on a misunderstanding. When you go alone, you are not truly alone. Pray and ask the Holy Spirit to prepare your heart and the heart of the person who has sinned.

Step 2. "But if he does not listen to you, take one or two more with you, so that by the mouth of two or three witnesses every fact may be confirmed" (Matt. 18:16). If the first step has been followed faithfully and there is no reconciliation, you should take two or three witnesses. These persons may be able to help persuade the offender to repent. Further, they ensure objectivity, safety, and fairness. The small number of individuals involved provides for continued confidentiality. The

Bible doesn't specify who should be chosen, but they should be mature and trustworthy believers who can keep a confidence. The witnesses are not there to prove a case, but to encourage reconciliation. It is not insignificant that the verses immediately following this section in Matthew 18 record the famous promise— "For where two or three have gathered together in My name, I am there in their midst" (20).

Step 3. "If he refuses to listen to them, tell it to the church; and if he refuses to listen even to the church, let him be to you as a Gentile and tax collector" (18:17). The thrust of the entire witness of Scripture is that biblical discipline is designed to avoid this final step which results in the withdrawing of fellowship from a member of the church. This final step is an awesome and dramatic step. The severing of ties with a fellow-member is never to be taken lightly.

Some people refer to this final step as ex-communication. It would be more appropriate to speak of it as quarantine. While the unrepentant person has cut themselves off from fellowship with the body of Christ, the desired result of this quarantine is to bring them to repentance. We have only two clear examples in the New Testament of the application of this final step of church discipline.

The first example is found in 2 Thessalonians 3. It is telling that one of the earliest examples of church discipline involved persons spreading dissension in the church. A negative, critical spirit had disrupted the fellowship and thus affected the ministry and witness of the church.

The second example in 1 Corinthians 5 deals with the matter of sexual sin. It appears that the church was not only aware of the sin, some had responded with arrogance (5:2). Some in Corinth believed themselves to be so spiritual that sins of the flesh were of no consequence to them. Paul instructs the church "to deliver such a one to Satan for the destruction of his flesh, that his spirit may be saved in the day of the Lord Jesus" (5:5). While the terminology is more striking in this instance, the desired result is the same and that is to save the spirit—full restoration. It seems likely that 2 Corinthians 2:6-8 indicates that the discipline had its desired results and the fallen member was restored to fellowship.

This final step is a designed to ensure the purity of the Bride and the effectiveness of Her witness to the world. Thus it is enacted because of a sinful act which is blatant, arrogant, unrepentant, and broadly known in the community, impacting both the fellowship and witness of the church.

DISCIPLINE AND CHURCH MEMBERSHIP

Discipline is not widely practiced today because church membership is not highly valued. Mark Dever writes, "*Membership* draws a boundary line around the church, marking the church off from the world. *Discipline* helps the church that lives inside that boundary line stay true to the very things that are cause for drawing the line in the first place."[2] "One of the first steps in exercising discipline, therefore, is to exercise greater care in receiving new members."[3]

We have so devalued church membership and

become so obsessed with numerical growth, that we have made it easier to join the church than a social club. We need to teach prospective members the biblical requirements for church membership and clearly lay out God's expectations for church members. It is difficult to practice healthy and restorative discipline when people are not taught what is expected of a member of the body of Christ.

God is serious about His bride and we should be too!

---

1   John Stott, *Confess Your Sins: The Way of Reconciliation* (Waco, TX: Word, 1974), 49.
2   Mark Dever, *What is a Healthy Church?* (Wheaton, ILL: Crossway Books, 2005), 101.
3   Ibid. 104.

CONNECTED COMMUNITY
DESIGNED FOR BALANCED GROWTH

Paula and I recently had the joy of having our seven grandchildren—ranging in age from seven months to six years—in our home for a brief visit. Since our children live at the far ends of the globe, we only see the grandbabies a couple of times a year. Each time we see them, we are amazed and overjoyed to see how they have grown. Not only are they getting bigger, they also are becoming more articulate, they are able to interact with others at a more mature level, and they are able to outperform their "papa" on most computer-driven games.

We expect our children to grow! We look for multiple signs and different categories of growth, such as size, speech, social skills, etc. I believe that Luke provides four excellent categories for balanced growth as he comments on the development of the boy Jesus. "And Jesus kept increasing in wisdom and stature, and in favor with God and men" (2:52). Jesus' growth was balanced including intellectual, physical, spiritual and social. As parents we desire to see growth in each of these areas and if they are lacking we become concerned and may consult a specialist to determine why these signs of healthy growth are missing.

But this book is about the church and not about children. We have already determined that the church is not a *building*, but a *body*. It is not a *place*, but a *people*. It is not an *organization*, but an *organism*. As a living organism, a body made up of living members, it is designed for growth. The tragedy is that we have become so accustomed to a lack of growth in many churches that we think it is the norm. Since the church is the body of Christ and the people through whom He has determined to advance His kingdom on earth, we must be willing to remove any barriers that inhibit the balanced growth of the church.

SUPERNATURALLY EMPOWERED FOR GROWTH

Let's make a brief stop in Caesarea Philippi and listen in on a private conversation between Jesus and His early disciples. Jesus first questions His followers concerning current speculation about His identity. But this question was only intended to prepare the way for a more critical question. Jesus wants to know what His followers had come to believe.

"But who do you say that I am?" (Matt. 16:15)

"Simon Peter answered, 'You are the Christ, the Son of the living God." (16:16).

"And Jesus said to him, 'Blessed are you, Simon Barjona, because flesh and blood did not reveal this to you, but My Father who is in heaven. I also say to you that you are Peter, and upon this rock I will build My church...'" (16:17-18b).

Not only does Jesus affirm Peter's conclusion that He is the Messiah, the Son of the one true living God, He announces His plan for expanding His kingdom to the ends of the earth by establishing and building His own church. I want you to underline the phrase "I will build." Jesus promised to build His church. The church is designed for growth! It is supernaturally empowered, enabling it to experience balanced growth.

If we fast forward to the account of the birth of the church at Pentecost, we will see that it has growth in its DNA. After his Pentecost message, Peter invited people to turn from their sin and receive the gift of the Holy Spirit (Acts 2:38). In verse 41 we notice that growth was immediate, natural, and supernatural. "So then, those who received his word were baptized; and that day there were added about three thousand souls." This great harvest was not an isolated phenomenon like the response at a Billy Graham crusade.

Other signs of healthy growth soon presented themselves. Early members of the church manifested a hunger for doctrinal teaching, a desire for fellowship with other believers, spontaneous generosity, and joyous worship (Acts 2:42-47). This balanced growth, in turn, led to regular and consistent numerical growth—"And the Lord was adding to their number day by day those who were being saved" (2:47b). The verb translated "was adding" is passive, indicating that "growth" was something God was accomplishing for and through the church at His own initiative.

I would invite and challenge you to read through the book of Acts looking for expressions that demonstrate the supernatural activity of the Spirit producing growth in the church. Let me help you get started. Peter and John are arrested for healing a man. They are threatened and released. When they report to the church what transpired, they gather for prayer with the result that the place is shaken and they speak the word of God with boldness (4:31). This story is followed by another summary description that pictures the generous fellowship of the church, the result of the abundant grace which was upon them all (4:34). Would someone describe your church with words like, "great power" and "abundant grace?"

The growth of the church created challenges which were nothing less than opportunities for the Spirit-empowered community. Acts 6:1 tells us that the rapid expansion of the church caused the Hellenistic Jews to complain about the service being afforded to their widows. The problem was quickly resolved and the results were immediate. "The word of God kept on spreading; and the number of the disciples continued to increase greatly in Jerusalem" (6:7a).

Paul, the greatest church planter of the first century, emphasized the natural and supernatural elements of growth in the church in his first letter to the Corinthians. Some of the immature Corinthians were enamored by the reputation of various early church leaders and wanted to boast about men. Paul responds by using himself and Apollos as examples. "I planted, Apollos watered, but God was causing the growth" (1 Cor. 3:6). Note that all growth is the result of supernatural activity. This, however, does not mean that men like Apollos and Paul are insignificant. In fact, they are the instrument through whom God caused the growth (3:5). God has chosen to grow His church by using human instruments and it is for this reason that Paul cautions readers of every age to be careful to build with the highest quality material (3:10-15).

Are you an instrument through whom God is at work building His church?

HEALTHY CHURCH GROWTH BEGINS WITH GROWING BELIEVERS

Since the church is a body of believers, it stands to reason that when individual members fail to grow spiritually the church will not grow as God intended. In Acts 11, Luke introduces us to one of the greatest churches of all times, the church at Antioch. In a span of eight verses Luke tells us three times that a large number of people were being evangelized and discipled by the church at Antioch (11:21, 24, and 26).

Phrases such as "hand of the Lord" (11:21) and "the grace of God" (11:23) describe the supernatural empowering of the church. When Barnabas is privileged to witness God's activity in this great church, he immediately brings Saul to Antioch. "And for an entire year they met with the church and taught considerable numbers; and the disciples were first called Christians in Antioch" (11:26). It is not insignificant that the Holy Spirit records that this discipling process took an "entire year." It underlines the commitment to spiritual growth among the leaders and participants in the early church.

It was the growth of the believers that created such generosity that the church sent an offering for the relief of the saints in Jerusalem. It was spiritual maturity that led the church to send Paul and Barnabas, two of their finest leaders, to plant churches throughout the known world (13:1-3). Personal spiritual growth and balanced church growth go hand in hand.

Thabiti Anyabwile describes the spiritual growth necessary for a healthy church. He writes that a healthy church member will show concern not only for their own personal growth but also for the growth of others. They will progressively and continually evidence the fruit of the Spirit in their life. They will desire to grow up in the stature of the fullness. In other words, they are growing to be more like Jesus in attitude, thought, speech, and action.[1] Does this describe most members of your church? Does it describe you?

A HEALTHY CHURCH GROWS IN CHARACTER

Every church has a personality or character and it is the sum-total of the character of its members. I encounter some churches that are known for their divisive spirit. Guess what? They have members who are divisive in nature. Some churches are known for their burden for the lost, for their mission spirit, or their generosity. Once again it is because they are composed of people who express these character traits in their lives both individually and corporately. If I were to ask people who live around your church about the character of your church, what would they say?

We can't ignore this issue of growth in character because God's eternal plan is to use the church as the canvas on which He displays his manifold wisdom. Paul indicates this is the eternal purpose which God carried out in sending Christ Jesus our Lord to earth (Eph. 3:10-11). God went to extreme ends to make it possible for the church to fully reflect His glory. He raised Jesus from the dead, seated Him at His right hand, put everything in subjection under His feet, and gave Him as head over everything for this singular purpose.

Are our churches growing in their likeness to Christ? When we grow in character, we will express God's heart for the downcast, the outcast, the hurting, and the lonely. A growing church will of necessity be missional in character because it reflects God's heart for the nations. If we are serious about being His church and expressing His fullness, we must ask, "Are we expressing God's character not only when we are gathered together but when we are scattered throughout the community?" We can ask this in another way. "Are we both salt and light for our community?" "Would our community miss our church if it was no longer here?"

A HEALTHY CHURCH EXPERIENCES BALANCED GROWTH

Some people avoid the topic of "church growth" because we have often reduced it to "nickels and noses"—a mere recitation of statics which are often padded to boost our human ego, as if belonging to the largest or fastest growing church indicates the level of our spirituality. While our concern for the lost must compel us to pray for and celebrate numerical growth, we must seek biblical and balanced growth and understand that God causes the increase.

The Ephesian letter is like a love letter to the church. We have already seen that Paul challenges the church to express God's manifold wisdom (3:10). He prays that the church—individually and corporately—

would be strengthened by the Holy Spirit, indwelt by Christ, know the love of Christ, and be filled up to the fullness of God (3:14-19).

In chapter 4 Paul explains how the church is designed to grow into the full measure of Christ. He begins first by calling believers to embrace the unity provided to the church by the work of the triune God in all members (1-6). He then proceeds to explain that each member is uniquely gifted by the risen Lord to participate in the growth of the church (7-10). Did you know that you are one of God's gifts to your church and that you are critical to its balanced growth?

Paul provides a brief sketch of how the gifted body works as gifted leaders equip gifted members for the work of service. When all the members function according to their unique gifts, it builds up the body of Christ "until we all attain to the unity of the faith, and of the knowledge of the Son of God, to a mature man, to the measure of the stature which belongs to the fullness of Christ" (13). This is balanced, biblical, natural, and supernatural growth. This is the growth that your church is designed and empowered to experience.

GOD IS GLORIFIED WHEN HIS CHURCH GROWS

Many church members recoil at the notion of growth because they like their church "the way it is." Growth will necessarily cause "change" and change is threatening and often uncomfortable. We enjoy the fellowship of our small group, the familiarity of our worship experience, and the comfort of "knowing everyone by name." So why would we want our church to grow? We have already suggested that we should desire our church to grow because it is both natural and healthy since the church was designed for growth. Further, concern for the lost mandates that we expand our ministries to include others. But the primary reason is that God is glorified when His church grows.

In his letters Paul reminds the churches that he is continually praying for them. One of my favorite Pauline prayers is the one recorded in Ephesians 3:14-21. Listen to the benediction—"Now to Him who is able to do far more abundantly beyond all that we ask or think, according to the power that works within us, to Him be the glory in the church and in Christ Jesus to all generations forever and ever. Amen." His promise of empowering enables us to do "abundantly beyond" all that we can imagine or pray for. He accomplishes this growth through divine empowering which is made available in and through us with the end result that He receives glory in the church and in Christ Jesus. When the church experiences healthy growth God is glorified.

When God accomplishes His work through your local church, He receives the glory. Attention is drawn to Him through His Son's bride. When He is glorified, He draws men to Himself which once again results in growth which brings glory to Him. Church growth is neither our goal nor our work. Our goal is to glorify God and He enables us to do so by working in us to grow His church. Wow!

---

1   Thabiti M. Anyabwile, *What is a Healthy Church Member?* (Crossway Books: Wheaton, ILL, 2008), 88-89.

CONNECTED COMMUNITY
PARTNERS IN GOD'S GLOBAL TASK

Several years ago, I followed a story with rapt fascination and concern. One whale after another was found lying helpless on a familiar stretch of beach. People were frantically trying to keep the whales alive until they could be shepherded back into the water. No one seemed to know what had caused these behemoths of the sea to swim close enough to the shore to become helplessly stranded in shallow water, fighting for survival.

The answer was both simple and telling. These mammoth creatures had been so busy pursuing small minnows that they had ignored the changing currents and shifting sandbars, resulting in their own potential demise.

I fear that the church may face the same danger as these whales. The church was created and empowered by God for reaching the nations, but we have become so obsessed chasing minnow-sized goals that we have ignored the changing currents of our time and lost sight of our mission. We are in danger of becoming like a beached and bloated whale in need of assistance for mere survival.

We know that 80% of evangelical churches are plateaued or declining and yet we spend more time debating minnow-sized issues such as the color of the carpet, style of music, or the time of services than we spend accomplishing the mission of the church. If we are to experience genuine revival and its resulting revitalization, we must repent of our minnow-mindset and embrace our God-given mission.

In the last chapter we looked at Paul's insistence that the church was designed and empowered to express God's fullness in the world today. God sent His only son to establish His church and to enable her to accomplish this goal. On two different occasions in the Ephesian letter, Paul prays passionately that believers will understand their calling and their empowering (1:18-23 and 3:14-21). In his benediction to the second prayer, he declares that God will do immeasurably more than we can ask or think through His church for His own glory. In light of the mammoth potential of the church, we must ask why we are accomplishing so little.

THE RESURRECTED KING— HIS KINGDOM AND HIS CHURCH

Luke begins his second volume (the book of Acts) with a reminder that in his first account he had told all that Jesus had done and taught up until He was taken up into heaven (Acts 1:1-2). He then speaks of the many convincing resurrection appearances and Jesus' continued teaching concerning the kingdom of God (3). Luke records this with such simplicity that we may be guilty of reading it so quickly that we miss the significance of the moment.

Can you imagine the impact of seeing the resurrected Lord? Grief turned to jubilation! Lingering doubt replaced with absolute confidence! It is now clear that Jesus is truly who He claimed to be. He is Messiah/King. He is the Only Begotten of the Father. He is the only Redeemer. He alone provides access to the Father. But Jesus didn't simply make an appearance to encourage His disciples, He continued to teach on that which had been the theme of His earthly ministry—the kingdom of God. No doubt He wanted them to understand its centrality and their role in expanding this kingdom. Jesus, the rightful King of all nations is transferring the keys of the kingdom to the church as He promised His disciples (Matt. 16:17-19).

The global and eternal significance of the moment make the question of Acts 1:6 seem to be a minnow-sized diversion. "Lord, is it at this time You are restoring the kingdom to Israel?" They were Jews and the hope of the restoration of Israel's national independence was still a high priority. But in comparison with the kingdom of God all such earthly issues were simply that—earthly. Jesus reminds them that the Father controls all events according to His own timetable and therefore they shouldn't get sidetracked with temporal issues when they had been called to a kingdom-sized task that will impact eternity. Does your church get so focused on temporal issues that it loses sight of its kingdom task?

Notice the strong adversative "but" that begins verse 8. We might paraphrase, "The Father has everything in control concerning all earthly events, *but* you have received the power to expand my kingdom to the ends of the earth." What an incredible promise! They are to receive power which will enable them to be

His witnesses starting in Jerusalem but encompassing the entire earth. They cannot become sidetracked with temporal concerns when they have been empowered to accomplish a ministry which will have eternal consequences. They are to advance His kingdom by His power and for His glory until His return.

Nothing has changed since the first century. The task is the same. The church is still God's chosen instrument for the advancing of His kingdom to the ends of the earth. We are still His witnesses. The empowering is still available through the Holy Spirit.

THE TASK OF THE CHURCH

Can you imagine what may have gone through the disciples' minds when Jesus declared that they are to be His witnesses to the ends of the earth (Acts 1:8)? When we hear the word "witness," we often think of those who are enrolled in the evangelism program of the church. "Witness" is first of all *who we are* before it is *what we do*. The early disciples had witnessed the resurrected Lord thus they had a story to tell. Anyone who has a personal relationship with the King is a *witness* and he/she has a story to *tell*. Being a witness will impact what we do and say. When *witnesses* do not tell their story, they are not simply being disobedient; they are denying who they are.

We may have unintentionally caused some confusion by describing evangelism as one of the tasks of the church. While I understand that the church has several functions, listing evangelism alongside those other functions may cause us to neglect the centrality of evangelism. When we view evangelism as one element of our work, we may see it as one of the programs of the church which may be selected or ignored by various members. For example, someone might say, "I a teach small group; evangelism is not my responsibility." Wrong! Evangelism is the privilege of every believer since all are witnesses. Each church must develop an intentional strategy for reaching their neighbor and the nations.

We must not forget that Matthew, Mark, and Luke all conclude their gospels with the mandate we refer to as the Great Commission (Matt. 28:19-20, Mark 16:15-16, and Luke 24:46-49). The first impulse of the disciples upon seeing Jesus is to worship Him as resurrected Lord (Matt. 28:18). Following this spontaneous act of worship, Jesus declares that the glorious, triumphant resurrection has secured for Him all authority in heaven and in earth (28:18 and cf. Eph. 1:18-23). The disciples are now commanded and given the power to take this message to the ends of the earth, making disciples of all nations.

Authentic worship naturally leads to passionate evangelism. When we are fully cognizant of what it means to worship the one true King, the only Savior, we will be compelled to share that message with all who have yet to hear that Good News. When a church takes the Great Commission as a "grand suggestion" and relegates the task of evangelism to the status of "one of our programs," evangelism is soon neglected or delegated to a "committed few." In turn, the church loses both its vitality and its passion for worship. It becomes focused on minnow-sized goals and finds itself beached and simply fighting for survival.

When a church corporately, and its people individually, keep their eyes on Jesus and His kingdom, conflict is avoided and we find purpose in our ministry. If you want to see your church revitalized, renew your focus on the mission given the church by its Lord.

POWER AND BOLDNESS

Luke, in his first volume, indicates that after Jesus commissioned His disciples to be His witnesses He instructed them to wait until they "are clothed with power from on high" (Lk. 24:49). Now in Acts 1:8 he tells us that the time of waiting is over and the time of empowering is now. As you read the book of Acts, you will find repeated references to the Holy Spirit giving the disciples boldness to witness.

One of the first examples of the power given for effective witness is the events which occurred at the celebration of Pentecost. Pentecost was celebrated fifty days after Passover. It was essentially a harvest celebration where God's people acknowledged Him as the source of rain and fertility (Jer. 5:24). It was called the "day of firstfruits" because it marked the beginning of the time when people brought offerings of their harvest to the Lord. Later tradition associated this feast with the giving of the law on Sinai. All able-bodied men were expected to be present at the sanctuary where a special sacrifice would be offered.

People from all the surrounding regions were present for the celebration. Meanwhile the disciples were together in one place waiting the empowering of the Spirit. Both visible and audible signs accompanied the descent of the Spirit causing the crowd to come together (Acts 2:6). They were astounded that they were able to hear the message in their own language. Peter seized the moment and, utilizing various Old Testament passages, he bore witness to Jesus. When the crowd heard the message, "they were pierced to the heart" (2:37). The Spirit not only guided Peter's thoughts, he brought conviction of sin to the hearers.

The healing of a lame man (ch. 3) provided another opportunity for Peter to be a witness. He simply deflected attention away from himself and to the true source of life. Once again he gives people the opportunity to respond to his words. "Therefore repent and return, so that your sins may be wiped away…" (3:19a).

Our task is to bear witness to the life-transforming power of Christ. It is the work of the Spirit to bring conviction and conversion. If you are a follower of Christ, you are a witness. The question is, "How credible are you as a witness?" Are you allowing the Holy Spirit to empower you for witness?

THE GLOBAL SCOPE OF OUR WITNESS

We must allow the King to determine the scope of our ministry. Too often churches assume they are too small to have much of an impact. Don't forget that the early church began with a small group of committed followers but were soon accused of "upsetting the world" (Acts 17:6). The mention of Jerusalem, Judea, Samaria, and the ends of the earth was not simply a picturesque way of speaking of the church's mission.

Jerusalem, Judea, Samaria, and the ends of the earth depict an ever increasing opportunity that crosses both regional and racial barriers. As you read the book of Acts you will notice that these four quadrants of concern actually outline the book of Acts and describe the church's activity. The early disciples had the audacity to believe that they could be witnesses to the ends of the earth.

The task remains unfinished and therefore is the responsibility and calling of the church today. The four quadrants of the Acts 1:8 mandate—Jerusalem (our community), Judea (our region), Samaria (our continent), and the ends of the earth (the known world)—must be engaged simultaneously. Further, churches will often discover that there are people from each of these quadrants now living in their community. Every local church must have a strategy for responding to the Acts 1:8 commission. This means we must get out of our four walls and our comfort zone. While we engage our community we must establish partnerships that will enable us to work with other like-minded kingdom churches to join in the reaching beyond our community.

If you think it is unreasonable to think that a local church could be so bold as to undertake a global mission, I would encourage you to read the story of the church at Antioch as told in Acts 11:19-30 and 13:1-3. This church was founded by laymen who had been scattered because of the persecution of the church in Jerusalem. This church grew rapidly because the "hand of the Lord was with them." They sensed the Holy Spirit calling them to a broader scope of ministry and thus sent Paul and Barnabas to the work which God called them. This was the beginning of the Pauline missionary journeys which led to the planting of most of the churches we read about in the New Testament. This church was willing to give their best leaders to plant other churches.

PRACTICAL SUGGESTIONS

Your church has the opportunity and the empowering to touch the nations and impact eternity. You must become intentionally missional. Let me make a few suggestions that can be applied by any church.

- *Pray.* Develop a strategic plan for praying for lost persons in your community, for specific mission personnel, and for unreached people groups.
- *Go.* Get out of the building. Start with a mission project in your community and then expand the scope of your mission involvement as the Lord allows.
- *Send.* Have a plan for mission's education for every age group. Challenge people to respond to the call to part-time and full-time missions.
- *Give.* We must give to those who are willing to plant their lives at "the ends of the earth." Individuals and churches should strive for a lifestyle that will allow them to give more than a mere 10% of their resources for reaching the lost in all four quadrants of the Acts 1:8 imperative.
- *Plant.* A missional church must reproduce itself by planting other like-minded congregations.

CONNECTED COMMUNITY
ASSURED OF VICTORY

What happens in and through your church has greater significance than that which occurs in the boardrooms of the Fortune 500 companies or in the halls of political power. These earthly institutions deal with *temporal* issues and the church deals with *eternal* issues. Your church is designed and empowered to advance God's kingdom by His power until His glorious return. You can be certain that Christ and His church will be triumphant.

The statement of ultimate victory may seem hard to believe when you look at the social and moral condition of your community, our nation, and the world. The family is under attack, marriages are in disarray, disobedience and outright rebellion are in evidence in every arena. Sexual immorality, drug abuse, and violence appear to rule the day from public schools to boardrooms. Social unrest, rampant terrorism, the proliferation of cults, and the advance of other world religions make the church look anything but triumphant.

Add to this, the general apathy exhibited toward spiritual matters and global evangelization by the average church and its members and it makes it a bit challenging to believe that the church as we know it is capable of advancing God's kingdom. Relatively few believers (some estimate less than 20%) make any significant investment of time, abilities, or money through their church for the sake of the kingdom. The average church in North America spends nearly 95% of its resources on its own members. A lack of progress has caused many churches to chase the latest fad to attract "prospects" and entertain their own members.

And all of this disappointing data must be cast on a global stage where 1.65 billion people have little or no access to the gospel. Some missiologists question whether the church in North America is capable of being a viable player in the global advance of God's kingdom. It is true that we can't continue to play at church and be a significant force in advancing God's kingdom. But we have the calling, the potential, and the empowering. We must turn our back on church games and become the church that God intended. I am still hopeful and so are you or you would not be engaged in this study.

THE BEGINNING OF THE END

The event we sometimes refer to as "The Triumphal Entry" appears to the unaided eye to be anything but triumphal. Jesus rides humbly into Jerusalem on a "borrowed" donkey (Jn. 12:12-19). Hardly what one would expect of a triumphant King. The general public, however, is fascinated because they have heard that Jesus raised Lazarus from the dead. Some Greeks (Gentiles) approach with a genuine desire to see Jesus. Jesus tells them of His glorification which, paradoxically, will be his death. Further, He tells them that if anyone desires to follow Him they must lose their own life and serve Him.

At this point in the proceedings, the Father audibly affirms that the Son has glorified His name. You may recall that the Father spoke from heaven at the inauguration of Jesus' ministry when Jesus submitted Himself to John's baptism (Matt. 3:17). In this instance some think they have heard thunder, while others think that an angel has spoken (Jn. 12:27-29). In this highly charged moment, Jesus declares: "Now judgment is upon this world; now the ruler of this world will be cast out. And I, if I am lifted up from the earth, will draw all men to Myself" (31-32).

The phrase "lifted up from the earth" probably refers to both the "lifting up" at the crucifixion and the resurrection. To the world, the crucifixion appeared to be Jesus' ultimate defeat. But the cross was actually Jesus' greatest victory and the death blow for Jesus' adversary the devil. Jesus' death is the only sufficient sacrifice for the sin of mankind and thus Satan's hold over sinful man is broken. Jesus had entered the strong man's house and had emerged triumphant (cf. Mark 3:27). At the moment Jesus was lifted up, the adversary's power was broken and his days were numbered.

Yet while Satan is a defeated foe, he is not yet banished from the earth. He now depends upon deception, confusion, and its resulting apathy to keep people from joining the advancing army composed of those who dare to identify with the King. Though our ultimate victory is assured, there yet remains a battle for men's souls and this is the task of the church. When we fully comprehend the context of our ministry we understand that too much is at stake for us to play at church!

CHRIST AT THE RIGHT HAND OF THE FATHER POURING OUT BLESSING

At this moment, even as you are reading these words, Christ rules and reigns from His royal position at the right hand of the Father. He is moving everything in history toward one final event—the judgment of the nations and the full and triumphant establishment of His kingdom. He is accomplishing His kingdom activity on earth through the community of the redeemed— His church, His glorious bride.

In the Colossian letter Paul describes in magnificent terms the work of Christ in the redemption of sinful man. He speaks of Christ transferring us from the domain of darkness to the kingdom of His beloved Son (1:13). After he speaks of the glory of Christ manifested in the creation of all things, he declares, "He is head of the body, the church; and He is the beginning, the firstborn from the dead, so that He Himself will come to have first place in everything" (1:18). While God's glory is revealed in creation, it is but a dim shadow of His glory when compared with His manifestation of Himself in His church. We cannot overlook the intentional linking of redemption, the church, and Christ's dominion over all things.

In Ephesians, the companion letter, Paul describes in great detail how God's glory is now manifested through His church. Paul allows us to visit his prayer closet as he intercedes for the churches of pro-Consular Asia. Not only does he give thanks to God for their faith in Christ and their love for the saints, He prays that they will have a spirit of wisdom and revelation (1:15-17). Simply stated, Paul wants them to go *deeper* so they can reach *higher*.

He prays that they will fully comprehend the "surpassing greatness of His power toward us who believe" (19). Don't miss this—the power available to the church is the same power which was at work when God raised His Son from the dead and established Him as head over all things (20-22). It gets better! "And He put all things in subjection under His feet, and gave Him as head over all things to the church, which is His body, the fullness of Him who fills all in all" (22-23).

The term translated "fullness" is the same term Paul used in Colossians 1:19 to describe Christ as the full expression of God. The Father's pleasure was to manifest His own fullness in Christ so that through Him he could reconcile all things to Himself (Col. 1:20). That same "fullness" is now made manifest in the world through the church, whose task it is to carry to full completion that ministry of reconciliation begun in Christ. This truth permeates the entire Ephesian letter.

In chapter 2 Paul speaks of man's redemption through grace which results in our re-creation enabling us to accomplish the good works that God prepared for us to do before time began (1-10). Did you know that you have a role to play in the kingdom advance of your church that God has designed specifically for you to accomplish? He created and redeemed you for this very purpose.

In the second half of chapter 2, Paul marvels at how God, through the cross of Christ, broke down the inner wall of partition that had separated Jew from

Gentile. Gentiles are now fellow-citizens with the saints and are members of God's household. They are built upon the foundation of the apostles and prophets, with Christ as the corner stone (2:20). This community, fitted together by God, is growing into a holy temple, a dwelling place of God in the Spirit (2:21-22).

In chapter 3 Paul speaks of his unique role in ministry to the Gentiles and the unveiling of a mystery which had been hidden from before the beginning of time by the One who created everything. Do you want to know the content of that mystery? "So that the manifold wisdom of God might now be made known through the church to the rulers and authorities in the heavenly places. This was in accordance with the eternal purpose which He carried out in Christ Jesus our Lord" (3:10-11).

Is it any wonder that Paul breaks forth in passionate prayer yet again as he contemplates the role of the church in redemptive history? He prays for power, the indwelling of Christ, the comprehension of the love of Christ so that they may be filled up to the fullness of God (3:14-19). Paul's benediction is one of passionate praise for the One who accomplishes more than we can ask or imagine by working "within us," His church. "To Him be the glory in the church and in Christ Jesus to all generations forever and ever" (3:21). When God receives glory through your church it is reflected back on His Son.

In chapter 4 Paul explains how the church, your church, can grow to express God's fullness. The exalted Lord gives gifts to individuals and then gives those gifted individuals to the church. As the pastors/

teachers equip the gifted saints for service the church is enabled to grow in unity, knowledge of the Son of God and to the maturity that belongs to the fullness of Christ (4:13). This message is so dear to Paul that his discussion of the relationship between a husband and wife quickly becomes a dissertation on the love Christ for His church (5:32).

Ephesians teaches us that Christ the King sits now on the right hand of the Father pouring out blessing upon His church to enable it to express His fullness in the world today.

HIS IMMINENT RETURN AND OUR CALL TO SERVICE

Speculation concerning Christ's return seems to be at a fever pitch this year. Tragically, many believers seem to be more fascinated about the date of His return than they are about the significance of His return.

The return of the Lord, while it will be a glorious event for believers, will be a sad and final day for those who do not know Christ as their Lord. When Jesus' own disciples asked about the sign of His coming and the end of the age, He responded by telling them not to be deceived or shaken by the signs they see unfolding in the world. He affirms that those who endure in following Him will be saved (Matt. 24:13). Further, He promises that the gospel of the kingdom will be preached in the whole world prior to His return (24:14).

He assures them that after the tribulation the Son of Man will appear in the sky with power and great glory. From this exalted position, He will send His angels to gather the elect from one end of the sky to the other (24:29-31). Jesus follows this teaching of His coming with several parables that affirm that the coming of the Lord will be sudden, unexpected, and terminal. Each parable stresses the need to be ready for His coming. Those who understand the coming of the Lord will be doing the task assigned by the Master when He comes (24:46). The parable of the ten virgins teaches that those who make preparation for His coming are those whom He knows (25:12). The parable of the talents (25:14-30) and the parable of the sheep and goats (25:31-46) teach us that our service to the King in this life matters in the life to come.

When the Thessalonian believers ask Paul about the time of the Lord's return, he responds that they do not need any additional information (1 Th. 5:1). Since they are not in darkness, they must remain alert and sober (5:6). Since we know that one day we will live together with Him, we must spend our earthly time encouraging and building up one another (5:10-11). In 2 Thessalonians the topic of the second coming is addressed once again with the exhortation that they must stand firm and hold to those things they have been taught (2 Th. 2:15).

Do you see the common thread in all these passages? We don't need to waste time speculating about Christ's return. Our mission in this generation is too important and our message is too critical for us to fail to encourage fellow believers so that together we can reach the nations. Every generation should view itself as the terminal generation and thus live with the passion of reaching the ends of the earth.

THE CHURCH COMING DOWN FROM HEAVEN

There are some beautiful images in the book of Revelation. In the fifth chapter, we see the twenty-four elders before the lamb singing a new song. Just listen—"Worthy are You to take the book and to break its seals; for You were slain, and purchased for God with Your blood men from every tribe and tongue and people and nation. You have made them to be a kingdom and priests to our God; and they will reign upon the earth" (5:9-10). The church has completed its task of taking the gospel of the kingdom to the ends of the earth.

In the final chapters we hear of the final demise of Satan and his followers who are cast into the lake of fire (20:10). In chapter 21 we are given a glimpse of the new heaven and earth. The key image is the dwelling of God with His people. The new Jerusalem comes down from heaven "made ready as a bride adorned for her husband" (21:2). It is the Spirit and the bride who bid those in Christ to "come" (22:17). The church, the perfected bride, is presented in purity and glory to Christ.

What you offer to God through your service to and through His church will be presented to the King in heaven.

iBELIEVE SERIES

If you've enjoyed thIs book in the iBelieve Series, you may want to watch for future books:

CERTIFIED TRUE:
TRUSTING THE BIBLE

EMPOWERED LIVING:
BEING FILLED BY THE HOLY SPIRIT

SECURED FOREVER:
ANTICIPATING LIFE AFTER DEATH

TRANSFORMED LIFE:
EXPERIENCING REDEMPTION

Coming soon from Auxano Press.

For CORE CONVICTIONS, the first book in the iBelieve Series, and other titles by Ken Hemphill, please visit auxanopress.com/catalog

FREE STUDY GUIDES for *Core Convictions* and *Connected Community* for 7- or 13-week study are available at AuxanoPress.com